Lincoln

ROY P. BASLER

OCTAGON BOOKS

A DIVISION OF FARRAR, STRAUS AND GIROUX

New York   1975

First published 1961
All Rights Reserved

Allen County Public Library
Ft. Wayne, Indiana

Reprinted 1975
by special arrangement with Roy P. Basler

OCTAGON BOOKS
A DIVISION OF FARRAR, STRAUS & GIROUX, INC.
19 Union Square West
New York, N.Y. 10003

Library of Congress Cataloging in Publication Data

Basler, Roy Prentice, 1906-
    Lincoln.

    Reprint of the 1961 ed. published by Grove Press, New York,
    which was issued as Evergreen profile book, 37.

    Bibliography: p.
    1. Lincoln, Abraham, Pres. U.S., 1809-1865.
[E457.B34   1975]   973.7'092'4 [B]   75-29365
ISBN 0-374-90454-5

Printed in USA by
Thomson-Shore, Inc.
Dexter, Michigan

To

The Family of Man

"Our defense is in the preservation of the spirit which prizes liberty as the heritage of all men, in all lands, everywhere." – Speech at Edwardsville, Illinois, September 11, 1858.

Lincoln statue by Daniel C. French, in the Lincoln Memorial Washington, D.C.

Lincoln
by Roy P. Basler

Contents

Lincoln Country

It was no accident that Abraham Lincoln, a rawboned, gangling giant, largely self-taught but as powerful in mind as in body, became the first Republican President of the United States at a time which required more than the common run of political talent and human energy to save the country which gave him birth. Nor was it an accident that his adversary Stephen A. Douglas, "the Little Giant" of the Democratic Party, was also a citizen of the same State of Illinois, in the same region, which was more "American" than any other section of their native land.

During the first half of the nineteenth century the area bounded by the Great Lakes on the north, the Mississippi on the west, and the Ohio River on the south and east was perhaps the single dominant factor in American politics: dominant in the economic development of the nation, and representative, even symbolic, of American civilization and culture, so that travelers from the Eastern Seaboard as well as from European countries recognized it as a "New World." During the first twenty-five years this area, then called the Northwest, or simply the West, was a frontier of American civilization in one or the other of two phases: the hunter and trader frontier, and the farmer frontier. By the time of the Civil War, however, it had acquired a relatively stable civilization.

Though predominantly agricultural, it was not notably more so than the areas east of the Appalachians or south of the Ohio, with the exception of those mercantile-

7

Lincoln as he appeared four days before the Gettysburg Address, November 15, 1863.

industrial areas centered in New England and the Middle Atlantic states which still had a lead on the expanding (almost exploding) mercantile-industrial centers along the Ohio and on the shore line of the Great Lakes. It had developed a characteristic system of public education which fostered not merely an average literacy equal to that of the older states, but also – in its new and as yet scarcely world-renowned colleges and universities – an intellectual leadership which commanded the respect of cultivated foreign travelers and occasionally compelled the attention of Boston or New York. It had developed, if not precisely the classless society that has so often been attributed to it, at least a society in which class distinctions were so flexible as to evade definition even by initiates, because the qualifications were so diverse: money, religion, education, family, and above all success – what kind of success did not matter too much so long as it was unmistakable. It had developed an audience which appreciated and was avid for literature, theater, music, and lyceum lectures of all kinds, although its first practitioners of the arts would not become recognized very widely for another two decades. However, in politics – the one activity of which all Americans of that era were purported master practitioners – the Northwest had produced a national leadership which could not be ignored.

2

In the only American tradition generally recognized at the time, the civilization of this area was to a considerable extent self made. But, like all things human, it had causes. Aside from physical geography, there was one principal cause which more than any other determined what kind of civilization developed in the area. This was the Northwest Ordinance of 1787 which provided for orderly settlement and the rapid establishment of new states. In summary, it may be said that the Ordinance undertook to insure to the people who settled the Northwest Territory not only the opportunity to form states equal to any others under the Constitution, but also the opportunity to escape, so far as possible under the Constitution and so far as the people's own wisdom would permit, from the vestiges of an aristocratic and feudal past which were firmly embedded in the society as well as in the constitutions of some of the older states – particularly slavery, primogeniture, and limitations on suffrage.

Prior to the passage of the Northwest Ordinance, England's cession of her claims to this territory by the Provisional Treaty of 1782 and the action of the several seaboard states in ceding their claims to the Federal government had set the stage for the young republic's first experiment in colonization by making it the first territory under jurisdiction of the Federal government. These were important acts. To the south of the Ohio two new states had been admitted to the Union, Kentucky in 1792 and Tennessee in 1796. In both, settlement had been retarded and early attempts at self-government had been frustrated by the parent states of Virginia and North Carolina, from which these new states were formed.

Although the majority of the pioneers who flooded into this western Virginia and North Carolina through the Appalachian valleys were not natives of either, and although they were for the most part politically and socially unsympathetic to the plantation system and to slavery, such was the hold of the Tidewater society on the government of the parent states that it was able to frustrate the effort in the West to adopt a radically different society or government. Land was disposed of

9

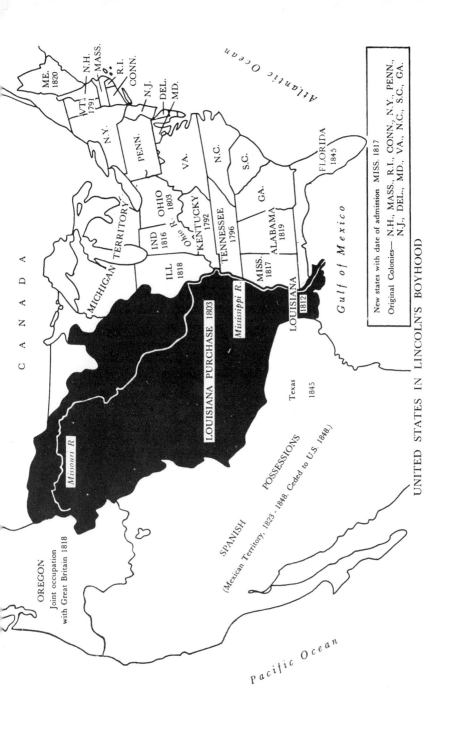

CANADA

ME. 1820

N.H.

MASS.

VT. 1791

R.I.

CONN.

N.Y.

N.J.

DEL.

MD.

PENN.

VA.

N.C.

FLORIDA 1845

MICHIGAN TERRITORY

OHIO 1803

S.C.

Ohio R.

IND 1816

KENTUCKY 1792

GA.

ILL 1818

TENNESSEE 1796

ALABAMA 1819

MISS. 1817

Mississippi R.

LOUISIANA PURCHASE 1803

LOUISIANA 1812

Gulf of Mexico

Atlantic Ocean

Missouri R.

Texas 1845

SPANISH POSSESSIONS

(Mexican Territory, 1823 - 1848. Ceded to U.S. 1848.)

OREGON
Joint occupation
with Great Britain 1818

Pacific Ocean

New states with date of admission MISS. 1817

Original Colonies— N.H., MASS., R.I., CONN., N.Y., PENN., N.J., DEL., MD., VA., N.C., S.C., GA.

UNITED STATES IN LINCOLN'S BOYHOOD

in lots of tremendous acreage in such a way as to encourage both speculation and the establishment of large plantation holdings and to discourage small farmers without slaves or to force them to become "squatters" without title. It is notable that although the constitutions of both Kentucky and Tennessee, unlike their parent states, granted suffrage to free men without property qualifications, both perpetuated slavery, and in addition Tennessee required property qualifications for its governor and members of its legislature, and also established a system of taxation favoring the wealthy plantation owner by limiting the taxation on slaves and setting the tax on land at a uniform rate without regard to the land's quality.

In contrast with this experience, the Northwest enjoyed not only the benefits of the Ordinance of 1787 but also a modicum of physical protection. It was Federal troops under Anthony Wayne and William Henry Harrison, dubiously assisted by frontier militia, that won the battles of Fallen Timbers and Tippecanoe. This protection so telescoped the first and second frontiers in the development of the Northwest that, unlike Kentucky and Tennessee, the Northwest never had a clearly established period of first settlements (except of course those of the French) entirely on their own against the wilderness and the savages. As a result, the rapid population of the Northwest by small farmers of modest means, who were from the beginning more or less permanent settlers rather than squatters or hunters, was to a considerable extent fostered if not actually subsidized by the Federal government.

This fact colored the peculiar blend of Republicanism and Federalism which became apparent in Ohio, Indiana, and Illinois, Jeffersonian in philosophy and Hamiltonian in allegiance. The typical political philosophy of the area – espoused by Buckeye, Hoosier, or Sucker, as the residents were called – recognized both the will of the people and the need for a strong Federal government to carry out that will. This is not to say that the settlers during the period of territorial government were of the opinion that the Federal government could govern them better as territories than they could govern themselves as states, but only that they recognized from the beginning that their power as a people derived from the nation rather than from the state. The citizenship they held in common both before and after achieving statehood was United States citizenship.

3

The essential goal of life in the West during the first half of the nineteenth century was the attainment of the greatest material prosperity, scientific advancement, and social progress that the world had ever known; a prosperity and progress for all, albeit any man who could lawfully attain more than another would be entitled to what he attained. There was enough for everybody and more for those who could get it. If his farm in Indiana was not as good as a man wanted, he could get a better one in Illinois. If the condition of laborer was not congenial, an ambitious man could read the law and go to practicing, or save a nest egg and become a capitalist himself.

Abraham Lincoln's advice on both possibilities was brief and to the point. In 1858 he wrote to a friend who had recommended a young man to study law with him: "When a man has reached the age that Mr. Widmer has, and has already been doing for himself, my judgment is, that he reads the books for himself without an instructor. That is precisely the way I came to the law." In an 1859 speech, while discussing the virtues of free versus slave labor, he admitted with pride: "Twenty-five years ago, I was a hired laborer. The hired laborer of yesterday, labors on his own account today; and will hire others to labor for him tomorrow. Advancement – improvement in condition – is the order of things in a society of equals."

It was just as simple as that to an ambitious man who had then lived forty-three of his fifty years in the Northwest. If one should object that there were few men of Lincoln's caliber in the Northwest at that time, the answer is that there were hundreds, perhaps thousands, who thought they were not merely equal to but, in the phrase of the time, "a damned sight better than" Lincoln. The important thing was that men thought it was so, and like Lincoln himself seldom missed a chance, whether in politics or other activities, to try to prove it.

In one of the campaign biographies of Abraham Lincoln known as "the Wigwam Edition," published in New York in 1860, the anonymous biographer introduced his subject as a backwoodsman.

If there is any one peculiarity of American nationality, any phase of American character by which it is distinguished in the eyes of discerning foreigners, any trait that will make it pre-eminent in history, it is that singular sort of energy, half physical and half intellectual, nervous, intense, untiring, which has achieved all of greatness that America has yet attained; . . . it is not delicate nor dainty, but tremendous and terrible; it is successful. This energy is manifested in many ways and by various characters, but by none more emphatically than the backwoods-man. . . .

The backwoods-man represents this individual American character. Abroad, the backwoods-man is looked upon, and rightly, as the representative American.

13

The only trouble with this designation of Abraham Lincoln as "backwoodsman" or "frontiersman" is that after his twenty-fifth year it was wholly inapplicable, and what was true of Lincoln was likewise true of most of his contemporaries in the Northwest; few of them were ever backwoodsmen for more than a short period of their lives, and the period of the frontier in the Northwest Territory was so fleeting as almost to seem an historical myth if one looks steadily at the life of any one man or at life in a particular community.

The communities which provided the cultural matrix of civilization in the new states of the Northwest were from the beginning well supplied with brains and an appreciation of the cultural ingredients that lend savor to civilization. Anyone who has studied the early history of a single community in the area, whether it be a community like Cincinnati, which rapidly became and re-

Cincinnati in 1855.

mained the leading metropolis of the area until overtaken after the Civil War by the younger cities on the Great Lakes, or a community like New Salem, Illinois, which disappeared within ten years after it was founded in 1829, cannot escape the evidence on every hand of the enormous energy referred to by the anonymous biographer of Lincoln. Although material necessities and comforts of life claimed a large share of this expenditure of energy, nevertheless, intellectual and spiritual activities flourished from the very beginning of each settlement. Churches, schools, subscription libraries, debating societies, lyceums, historical societies, museums, scientific societies, newspapers, and literary magazines were established as soon as, and in many instances earlier than, the mills, factories, and commercial establishments which largely supplanted frontier home manufacture and handicraft almost before the latter became an established

economy. In the intellectual sphere, the product was first of all for local consumption, of course, and was an inadequate fare which had to be supplemented by large importations from the East and from abroad, but there was an occasional item for export, such as Abolitionism, which shook the nation to its foundations.

What the citizen of the West thought of himself is abundantly recorded; two short and typical comments may suffice as brief examples. An anonymous Illinois correspondent of a Philadelphia newspaper wrote in 1837: "Assuming this fact as granted [that everyone must be the architect of his own fortune] I would refer to the superiority of the western portion of our continent over the eastern, as regards the *acquisition of wealth – professional eminence – political distinction,* and the opportunity offered of *exercising influence on society* and the *destinies of our common country.*" In the same vein spoke editor James Hall, whose *Illinois Monthly Magazine,* though certainly not the literary equal of *The North American Review,* was yet quite able to hold its own with most literary and intellectual organs of the East during the year 1830-1835: "The fact is that persons who emigrate to the west, have to learn from our people here, a vast deal more than they can possibly teach them." This confidence may have appeared to the Easterner, who frequently confused sophistication with education, as being somewhat overblown, but the emigrant to the West could ignore the advice only at great peril to his own success. The Bostonians as well as the Charlestonians had to "acknowledge the corn," to use a Western phrase of the period, when men like Abraham Lincoln and Stephen A. Douglas went east to represent their state in the Congress and the Senate during the next two decades.

"The Present Subject"

In spite of the most assiduous research carried on by a legion of writers for a full century, there is little that

can be added to the essential facts of Abraham Lincoln's early life as he wrote them down in June, 1860, shortly after his nomination as Republican candidate for the Presidency of the United States. This sketch of "the present subject," just as he wrote it except for minor editorial emendations, reads as follows:

Abraham Lincoln was born February 12, 1809, then in Hardin, now in the more recently formed County of Larue, Kentucky. His father, Thomas, and grandfather, Abraham, were born in Rockingham County, Virginia, whither their ancestors had come from Berks County,

17

Lincoln as a flatboatman (woodcut in Ward H. Lamon's Life of Abraham Lincoln, *1872).*

Pennsylvania. His lineage has been traced no farther back than this. The family were originally Quakers, though in later times they have fallen away from the peculiar habits of that people. The grandfather Abraham, had four brothers – Isaac, Jacob, John and Thomas. So far as known, the descendants of Jacob and John are still in Virginia. Isaac went to a place near where Virginia, North Carolina, and Tennessee, join; and his descendants are in that region. Thomas came to Kentucky, and after many years, died there, whence his descendants went to Missouri. Abraham, grandfather of the subject of this sketch, came to Kentucky, and was killed by Indians about the year 1784. He left a widow, three sons and two daughters. The eldest son, Mordecai, remained in Kentucky till late in life, when he removed to Hancock County, Illinois, where soon after he died, and where several of his descendants still reside. The second son, Josiah, removed at an early day to a place on Blue River, now within Harrison [Hancock] County, Indiana; but no recent information of him, or his family, has been obtained. The eldest sister, Mary, married Ralph Crume and some of her descendants are now known to be in Breckenridge County, Kentucky. The second sister, Nancy, married William Brumfield, and her family are not known to have left Kentucky, but there is no recent information from them. Thomas, the youngest son, and father of the present subject, by the early death of his father, and very narrow circumstances of his mother, even in childhood was a wandering laboring boy, and grew up literally without education. He never did more in the way of writing than to bunglingly sign his own name. Before he was grown, he passed one year as a hired hand with his uncle Isaac on Watauga, a branch of the Holston

18

River. Getting back into Kentucky, and having reached his 28th. year, he married Nancy Hanks – mother of the present subject – in the year 1806. She also was born in Virginia; and relatives of hers of the name of Hanks, and of other names, now reside in Coles, in Macon, and in Adams Counties, Illinois, and also in Iowa. The present subject has no brother or sister of the whole or half blood. He had a sister, older than himself, who was grown and married, but died many years ago, leaving no child. Also a brother, younger than himself, who died in infancy. Before leaving Kentucky he and his sister were sent for short periods, to A.B.C. schools, the first kept by Zachariah Riney, and the second by Caleb Hazel.

At this time his father resided on Knob-creek, on the road from Bardstown, Kentucky, to Nashville,

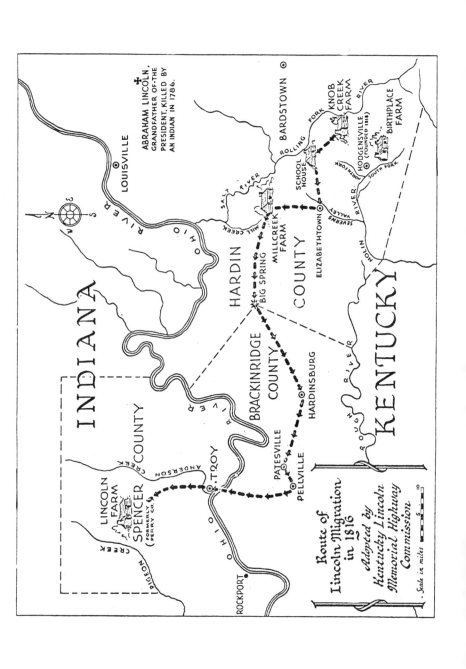

Tennessee, at a point three, or three and a half miles South or South-West of Atherton's ferry on the Rolling Fork. From this place he removed to what is now Spencer County, Indiana, in the autumn of 1816, Abraham then being in his eighth year. This removal was partly on account of slavery; but chiefly on account of the difficulty in land titles in Kentucky. He settled in an unbroken forest; and the clearing away of surplus wood was the great task ahead. Abraham though very young, was large of his age, and had an axe put into his hands at once; and from that till within his twentythird year, he was almost constantly handling that most useful instrument – less, of course, in plowing and harvesting seasons. At this place Abraham took an early start as a hunter, which was never much improved afterwards. (A few days before the completion of his eighth year, in the absence of his father, a flock of wild turkeys approached the new log-cabin, and Abraham with a rifle gun, standing inside, shot through a crack, and killed one of them. He has never since pulled a trigger on any larger game.) In the autumn of 1818 his mother died; and a year afterwards his father married Mrs. Sally Johnston, at Elizabeth-Town, Kentucky – a widow, with three children of her first marriage. She proved a good and kind mother to Abraham and is still living in Coles County, Illinois. There were no children of this second marriage. His father's residence continued at the same place in Indiana, till 1830. While here Abraham went to A.B.C. schools by littles, kept successively by Andrew Crawford, James Swaney, and Azel W. Dorsey. He does not remember any other. The family of Mr. Dorsey now reside in Schuyler County, Illinois. Abraham now thinks that the aggregate of all his schooling did not amount to one year. He was never

21

in a college or academy as a student; and never inside of a college or academy building till since he had a law-license. What he has in the way of education, he has picked up. After he was twentythree, and had separated from his father, he studied English grammar, imperfectly of course, but so as to speak and write as well as he now does. He studied and nearly mastered the Six-books of Euclid, since he was a member of Congress. He regrets his want of education, and does what he can to supply the want. In his tenth year he was kicked by a horse, and apparently killed for a time. When he was nineteen, still residing in Indiana, he made his first trip upon a flat-boat to New-Orleans. He was a hired hand merely; and he and a son of the owner, without other assistance, made the trip. The nature of part of the cargo-load, as it was called – made it necessary for them to linger and trade along the Sugar coast – and one night they were attacked by seven negroes with intent to kill and rob them. They were hurt some in the melee, but succeeded in driving the negroes from the boat, and then "cut cable" "weighed anchor" and left.

Leaving Lincoln's sketch for a moment, we may add a few points turned up by later biographers. The Lincoln genealogy has been accurately traced to Samuel Lincoln, a weaver's apprentice who migrated from Hingham, Norfolk, England, to Hingham, Massachusetts, in 1637. Samuel's grandson, Mordecai, migrated via New Jersey to Pennsylvania, where his son John Lincoln was born in 1716. John's son Abraham, for whom the grandson was named in 1809, was born not in Virginia as Lincoln supposed but in Pennsylvania, and accompanied his father to Rockingham County, Virginia.

On his mother's side, Lincoln's genealogy has never

Lincoln home in Indiana as it appeared in later years.

been completely clarified, in part because of incomplete records and in part because his mother Nancy Hanks was reputedly an illegitimate child. A great deal of controversy about this subject has appeared in print, from which two positive deductions can be made: Lincoln was aware himself of the gossip about his mother's birth; intensive and extensive research has not been able to certify the contrary beyond doubt. At any rate Lincoln's mother, Nancy Hanks, bore the maiden name of her mother, Lucy Hanks.

In regard to Lincoln's early education, or as he phrased it in all humility "his want of education," it should be pointed out that "the aggregate" amounting to one year would mean several years of short terms, as was customary in rural areas, whether east or west of the Appalachians. Furthermore, the only surviving objective evidence of this schooling, in the form of pages torn from a notebook which he kept in school at the age of fifteen or sixteen (1824-1826) shows conclusively that he

wrote well and did arithmetic accurately – a minimum not always achieved by high school graduates in our own century. His early interest in literary effort is likewise attested by the presence, scribbled over and among the arithmetic problems, of verses which have never been traced to any other source and may be assumed to have been, in part if not wholly, the products of his own youthful imagination, such as:

> Time what an empty vapor 'tis
> and days how swift they are
> swift as an Indian arrow
> fly on like a shooting star.

Undoubtedly many of the most important influences of his entire life came to bear on the boy Lincoln during these formative years, but it is mere speculation to pick out of his own meager allusions, or the not too reliable reminiscences collected by his former law partner William H. Herndon after Lincoln's death, those events which molded his personality. Plenty of hard work, which he was reputed to have said in later years his father taught him to perform but never to love, toughened a wiry, rangy body that reached a height of six feet four inches. But with seasonal changes, farm life provided interludes to the labor of wielding ax or hoe.

With his sister Sarah and later his stepbrothers and stepsisters, as well as children of neighboring settlers, the boy amused himself at the folk games and contests common to children. His penchant for social conversation, humorous anecdotes, and mimicry began to show, and he was credited with the usual "practical jokes" and "devilment" in which boys indulge. His familiarity with animals, particularly the domestic ones – hogs, chickens, cattle, horses – which later illustrated many of his hu-

morous stories, was acquired inevitably, as was his aware-
ness of the physical and mental habits and quirks of the
human species, for which no man ever demonstrated
a more sympathetically humorous understanding and
tolerance.

His mother's death of what was known as the "milk
sickness" when he was nine years old cannot have been
less than devastating. He and others said so little about
his mother, that only imagination can fill in the picture.
This is why Nancy Hanks is almost pure legend and
appears to more advantage in fictional accounts of Lincoln's boyhood than in strict biography. It does not
require much imagination, however, to picture the
desolate Lincoln cabin without her during the long winter
that followed her death or during the weeks a year later
when ten-year-old Abraham and his twelve-year-old sister
Sarah were left to keep house while their father returned
to Kentucky to marry the widow Johnston and fetch her
and her three children home to make a new family. If
his melancholy, which was forever after the obverse of
his humorous side, had to have a beginning this side of
his birth, one need go back no further for its source.

Lincoln's account continues as follows:

March 1st. 1830 – Abraham having just completed
his 21st. year, his father and family, with the families
of the two daughters and sons-in-law, of his step-
mother, left the old homestead in Indiana, and came
to Illinois. Their mode of conveyance was waggons
drawn by ox-teams, and Abraham drove one of the
teams. They reached the County of Macon, and
stopped there some time within the same month of
March. His father and family settled a new place on
the North side of the Sangamon river, at the junction
of the timber-land and prairie, about ten miles Westerly

from Decatur. Here they built a log-cabin, into which they removed, and made sufficient of rails to fence ten acres of ground, fenced and broke the ground, and raised a crop of sow[n] corn upon it the same year. These are, or are supposed to be, the rails about which so much is being said just now, though they are far from being the first, or only rails ever made by Abraham.

The sons-in-law, were temporarily settled at other places in the county. In the autumn all hands were greatly afflicted with ague and fever, to which they had not been used, and by which they were greatly discouraged – so much so that they determined on leaving the county. They remained however, through the succeeding winter, which was the winter of the very celebrated "deep snow" of Illinois. During that winter, Abraham together with his stepmother's son, John D. Johnston, and John Hanks, yet residing in Macon County, hired themselves to one Denton Offutt, to take a flat boat from Beardstown, Illinios to New-Orleans; and for that purpose, were to join him – Offutt – at Springfield, Illinois so soon as the snow should go off. When it did go off, which was about the 1st. of March 1831 – the county was so flooded, as to make traveling by land impracticable; to obviate which difficulty they purchased a large canoe and came down the Sangamon river in it. This is the time and the manner of Abraham's first entrance into Sangamon County. They found Offutt at Springfield, but learned from him that he had failed in getting a boat at Beardstown. This lead to their hiring themselves to him at $12 per month, each; and getting the timber out of the trees and building a boat at old Sangamon Town on the Sangamon river, seven miles N.W. of Springfield, which boat they took to New-

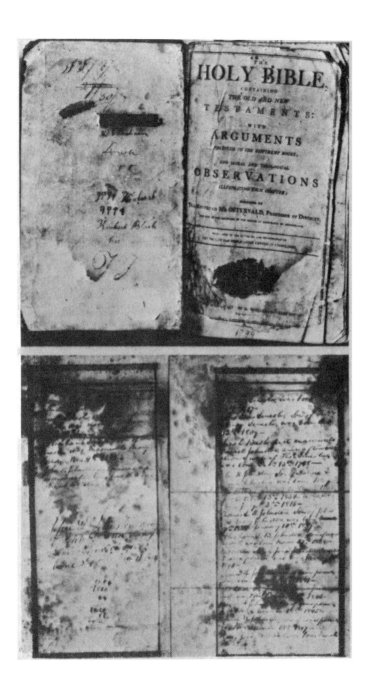

Family Bible containing Lincoln's record of the family genealogy.

Orleans, substantially upon the old contract. It was in connection with this boat that occurred the ludicrous incident of sewing up the hogs' eyes. Offutt bought thirty odd large fat live hogs, but found difficulty in driving them from where he purchased them to the boat, and thereupon conceived the whim that he could sew up their eyes and drive them where he pleased. No sooner thought of than decided, he put his hands, including Abraham at the job, which they completed – all but the driving. In their blind condition they could not be driven out of the lot or field they were in. This expedient failing, they were tied and hauled on carts to the boat. It was near the Sangamon River, within what is now Menard County.

Leaving Lincoln's sketch again for the moment, we may comment on this episode of driving the hogs. Why Lincoln should have narrated it in detail, as of sufficient import to include in so brief a sketch of his early life, no doubt puzzled his early biographers. It was omitted, with sound political instinct, from the campaign biographies for which he prepared this sketch, and on the specific instructions of his son, Robert Todd Lincoln, was omitted by his official biographers and editors, John G. Nicolay and John Hay, from their biography and their edition of his works. Certainly Lincoln's appreciation of the indelibly ridiculous was stronger during all periods of his life than was usual on the part of many squeamish contemporaries, and his lack of over-sensitivity on points of conduct – as opposed to points of morals – which would show him in something less than dignity, is attested many times over in anecdotes which he told at his own expense. Likewise, the episode was well known to his friends, as an integral part of this second flatboat trip to New Orleans, which was certainly important in itself; and to have left the episode out might have laid Lincoln open to the charge of "covering up." Few public figures have been more consistently candid about their personal lives.

It is interesting, in contrast, to observe that Lincoln included nothing about his observations of slavery at first hand on either of his two trips to New Orleans, although on both trips he had plenty of opportunity, and an episode in which he was alleged to have watched a New Orleans slave auction with deep personal revulsion was inserted into this story by his cousin John Hanks, who accompanied Lincoln and Johnston only as far as St. Louis and hence could not have witnessed the episode, if it in fact occurred. The fight with the seven Negroes, encountered on the first trip, is the only known incident in which Lincoln referred to slaves until he came as a politician to consider the evil of slavery as a moral and political problem. But to continue with Lincoln's sketch:

During this boat enterprize acquaintance with Offutt, who was previously an entire stranger, he conceived a liking for Abraham and believing he could turn him to account, he contracted with him to act as clerk for him, on his return from New-Orleans, in charge of a store and mill at New-Salem, then in Sangamon, now in Menard County. Hanks had not gone to New-Orleans, but having a family, and being likely to be detained from home longer than at first expected, had turned back from St. Louis. He is the same John Hanks who now engineers the "rail enterprize" at Decatur; and is a first cousin to Abraham's mother. Abraham's father, with his own family and others mentioned, had, in pursuance of their intention, removed from Macon to Coles County. John D. Johnston, the step-mother's son, went to them;

29

and Abraham stopped indefinitely, and, for the first time, as it were, by himself at New-Salem, before mentioned. This was in July 1831. Here he rapidly made acquaintances and friends. In less than a year Offutt's business was failing – had almost failed – when the Black-Hawk war of 1832 – broke out. Abraham joined a volunteer company, and to his own surprize, was elected captain of it. He says he has not since had any success in life which gave him so much satisfaction. He went the campaign, served near three months, met the ordinary hardships of such an expedition, but was in no battle. He now owns in Iowa, the land upon which his own warrants for this service, were located. Returning from the campaign, and encouraged by his great popularity among his immediate neighbors, he, the same year, ran for the Legislature

Diorama of Lincoln store. His customer is Ann Rutledge.

and was beaten – his own precinct, however, casting its votes 277 for and 7 against him. And this too while he was an avowed Clay man, and the precinct the autumn afterwards, giving a majority of 115 to General [Andrew] Jackson over Mr. [Henry] Clay. This was the only time Abraham was ever beaten on a direct vote of the people. He was now without means and out of business, but was anxious to remain with his friends who had treated him with so much generosity, especially as he had nothing elsewhere to go to. He studied what he should do – thought of learning the black-smith trade – thought of trying to study law – rather thought he could not succeed at that without a better education. Before long, strangely enough, a man offered to sell and did sell, to Abraham and another as poor as himself, an old stock of goods

upon credit. They opened as merchants; and he says that was *the* store. Of course they did nothing but get deeper and deeper in debt. He was appointed Postmaster at New-Salem – the office being too insignificant, to make his politics an objection. The store winked out. The Surveyor of Sangamon, offered to depute to Abraham that portion of his work which was within his part of the county. He accepted, procured a compass and chain, studied Flint, and Gibson a little, and went at it. This procured bread, and kept soul and body together. The election of 1834 came, and he was then elected to the Legislature by the highest vote cast for any candidate. Major John T. Stuart, then in full practice of the law, was also elected. During the canvass, in a private conversation he encouraged Abraham to study law. After the election he borrowed books of Stuart, took them home with him, and went at it in good earnest. He studied with nobody. He still mixed in the surveying to pay board and clothing bills. When the Legislature met, the law books were dropped, but were taken up again at the end of the session. He was re-elected in 1836, 1838, and 1840. In the autumn of 1836 he obtained a law licence, and on April 15, 1837 removed to Springfield, and commenced the practice, his old friend, Stuart taking him into partnership. March 3rd. 1837, by a protest entered upon the Illinois House Journal of that date, at pages 817, 818, Abraham with Dan Stone, another representative of Sangamon, briefly defined his position on the slavery question; and so far as it goes, it was then the same that it is now. The protest is as follows –

Resolutions upon the subject of domestic slavery having passed both branches of the General Assembly at its present session, the undersigned hereby protest against the passage of the same.

They believe that the institution of slavery is founded on both injustice and bad policy; but that the promulgation of abolition doctrines tends rather to increase than to abate its evils.

They believe that the Congress of the United States has no power, under the constitution, to interfere with the institution of slavery in the different States.

They believe that the Congress of the United States has the power, under the constitution, to abolish slavery in the District of Columbia; but that that power ought not to be exercised unless at the request of the people of said District.

The difference between these opinions and those contained in the said resolutions, is their reason for entering this protest.   Dan Stone
                                                                                                                     A. Lincoln

In 1838, and 1840 Mr. Lincoln's party in the Legislature voted for him as Speaker; but being in the minority, he was not elected. After 1840 he declined a re-election to the Legislature. He was on the Harrison electoral ticket in 1840, and on that of Clay in 1844, and spent much time and labor in both those canvasses. In November 1842 he was married to Mary, daughter of Robert S. Todd, of Lexington, Kentucky. They have three living children, all sons – one born in 1843, one in 1850, and one in 1853. They lost one, who was born in 1846.

At this point we must leave Lincoln's account in order to attempt to flesh out the portrait of a young man who had assumed full stature.

The Certainty of Uncertainty

After he left his father's home in March, 1831, Lincoln seems to have maintained only infrequent communication and to have made rare visits to that household. Although relations were cordial, the widening of his own horizon – intellectually, economically, and socially – left but little common ground on which to meet his family. His father remained a respected if impecunious farmer, and the family continued to live in much the same pattern as Lincoln had always known it. A dual letter written to his father and his stepbrother John D. Johnston while Lincoln was a Member of Congress tells in brief a story which needs no further amplification.

Washington, Decr. 24th. 1848 –

My dear father:

Your letter of the 7th. was received night before last. I very cheerfully send you the twenty dollars, which sum you say is necessary to save your land from sale. It is singular that you should have forgotten a judgment against you; and it is more singular that the plaintiff should have let you forget it so long, particularly as I suppose you have always had property enough to satisfy a judgment of that amount. Before you pay it, it would be well to be sure you have not paid it; or, at least, that you can not prove you have paid it. Give my love to Mother, and all the connections.

Affectionately your Son

A. Lincoln

The Statehouse in Springfield, Illinois, built as a result of Lincoln's political maneuvers.

Dear Johnston:

Your request for eighty dollars, I do not think it best, to comply with now. At the various times when I have helped you a little, you have said to me "We can get along very well now" but in a very short time I find you in the same difficulty again. Now this can only happen by some defect in your *conduct*. What that defect is, I think I know. You are not *lazy,* and still you *are* an *idler.* I doubt whether since I saw you, you have done a good whole day's work, in any one day. You do not very much dislike to work; and still you do not work much, merely because it does not seem to you that you could get much for it. This habit of uselessly wasting time, is the whole difficulty; and it is vastly important to you, and still more so to your children that you should break this habit. It is more important to them, because they have longer to live, and can keep out of an idle habit before they are in it; easier than they can get out after they are in.

You are now in need of some ready money; and what I propose is, that you shall go to work, "tooth and nails" for some body who will give you money for it. Let father and your boys take charge of things at home – prepare for a crop, and make the crop, and you go to work for the best money wages, or in discharge of any debt you owe, that you can get. And to secure you a fair reward for your labor, I now promise you, that for every dollar you will, between this and the first of next May, get for your own labor, either in money, or in your own indebtedness, I will then give you one other dollar. By this, if you hire yourself at ten dollars a month, from me you will get ten more, making twenty dollars a month for your work. In this, I do not mean you shall go off to St. Louis, or the lead mines, or the gold mines, in

California, but I mean for you to go at it for the best wages you can get close to home in Coles county. Now if you will do this, you will soon be out of debt, and what is better, you will have a habit that will keep you from getting in debt again. But if I should now clear you out, next year you will be just as deep in as ever. You say you would almost give your place in Heaven for $70 or $80. Then you value your place in Heaven very cheaply for I am sure you can with the offer I make you get the seventy or eighty dollars for four or five months work. You say if I furnish you the money you will deed me the land, and, if you don't pay the money back, you will deliver possession. Nonsense! If you can't now live *with* the land, how will you then live without it? You have always been kind to me, and I do not now mean to be unkind to you. On the contrary, if you will but follow my advice, you will find it worth more than eight times eighty dollars to you.

Affectionately Your brother   A. Lincoln

In New Salem, Lincoln twice fell in love, perhaps not for the first time, but with sufficient impact in both instances for these affairs to become a matter of record. A great deal of romantic reminiscence revolved around the reputedly beautiful Ann Rutledge more than a quarter of a century later, when in 1865-1867 a few of Lincoln's surviving friends and neighbors of the New Salem period were queried by Lincoln's erstwhile law partner and biographer, William H. Herndon. She was the daughter of James Rutledge, one of the founders of New Salem, at whose tavern Lincoln had lodged briefly upon first coming to the village. She died during the summer of 1835, probably of typhoid fever, and according to Herndon, Lincoln's only true love went with her into the

grave. Out of Herndon's story grew a sentimental legend which has been embroidered over and over in fiction and verse, in spite of the fact that Lincoln seems never to have mentioned her to his family or friends in later years. Even the members of her own generation recollected her chiefly as the result of Herndon's insistent prodding. Herndon made the most of this episode in order to provide his hero with a romantic love, which Herndon believed could not have existed in Lincoln's eventual marriage, for reasons which will become clear later.

Concerning Lincoln's second New Salem love affair, with Mary Owens, the facts are both clearer and less romantic, largely because Mary Owens kept the letters Lincoln wrote to her while attending the legislature, first at Vandalia and later at Springfield – which became the new capital of Illinois in February, 1837, as a result of Lincoln's successful logrolling in favor of the more centrally located village. Although only one side of this correspondence is preserved, it shows Lincoln to have been at first more interested than the not-so-young lady, and later, afraid that he was honor-bound although his heart had gone out of the affair. It is not surprising that their correspondence ended with the following letter:

Springfield Aug. 16th. 1837

Friend Mary.

You will, no doubt, think it rather strange, that I should write you a letter on the same day on which we parted; and I can only account for it by supposing, that seeing you lately makes me think of you more than usual, while at our late meeting we had but few expressions of thoughts. You must know that I can not see you, or think of you, with entire indifference; and yet it may be, that you, are mistaken in regard

39

Globe Tavern, where the Lincolns boarded after marriage. Photographed 1865.

to what my real feelings towards you are. If I knew
you were not, I should not trouble you with this letter.
Perhaps any other man would know enough without
further information; but I consider it *my* peculiar right
to plead ignorance, and your bounden duty to allow
the plea. I want in all cases to do right, and most
particularly so, in all cases with women. I want, at
this particular time, more than any thing else, to do
right with you, and if I *knew* it would be doing right,
as I rather suspect it would, to let you alone, I would
do it. And for the purpose of making the matter as plain
as possible, I now say, that you can now drop the subject, dismiss your thoughts (if you ever had any) from
me forever, and leave this letter unanswered, without

calling forth one accusing murmur from me. And I will even go further, and say, that if it will add any thing to your comfort, or peace of mind, to do so, it is my sincere wish that you should. Do not understand by this, that I wish to cut your acquaintance. I mean no such thing. What I do wish is, that our further acquaintance shall depend upon yourself. If such further acquaintance would contribute nothing to your happiness, I am sure it would not to mine. If you feel yourself in any degree bound to me, I am now willing to release you, provided you wish it; while, on the other hand, I am willing, and even anxious to bind you faster, if I can be convinced that it will, in any considerable degree, add to your happiness. This, in-

41

deed, is the whole question with me. Nothing would make me more miserable than to believe you miserable – nothing more happy, than to know you were so.

In what I have now said, I think I can not be misunderstood; and to make myself understood, is the only object of this letter.

If it suits you best to not answer this – farewell – a long life and a merry one attend you. But if you conclude to write back, speak as plainly as I do. There can be neither harm nor danger, in saying, to me, any thing you think, just in the manner you think it.

My respects to your sister.   Your friend Lincoln.

While perhaps not exactly a gay young blade in Springfield society, Lincoln took an active part in various organized activities, attending lyceum meetings, serving on cotillion committees, and going to barbecues and box suppers where eligible bachelors were in much demand. On some such occasion he met Mary Todd, a plump, vivacious young lady whose ambitions were no less demanding than his own, albeit not so concentrated in the realm of politics. A belle from Lexington, Kentucky, who had come to live with her sister, whose husband Ninian W. Edwards was one of Lincoln's close associates in Whig politics, Mary Todd had all the background of family prestige and education (including excellent French) that Lincoln lacked. As Lincoln was reputed to have remarked, one *d* was sufficient for God, but two were required for Todd, and so it was in other matters. Mary made no bones about the fact that she saw in Lincoln not simply a mate but a future, and for maintaining this feminine intuition in spite of what might have seemed on occasion overwhelming evidence to the contrary, she deserves not a little credit. In 1840 they became engaged.

Earliest portraits of Abraham and Mary Todd Lincoln (daguerreotypes ca. *1846-1847).*

Lincoln's uncertainty of his true feelings in regard to Mary Owens is understandable enough. With Mary Todd he reached a similar quandary within a few months, and on January 1, 1841, their engagement was broken. Just what took place cannot be completely recovered from the existing records, but, quite properly, their friends generally believed Lincoln had been jilted, and Lincoln's actions more than corroborated their belief. He lapsed into a depression so severe that he feared for his own sanity. On January 20, he wrote to his law partner then in Congress, John T. Stuart, a cousin of Mary Todd, asking that he obtain the appointment of Dr. Anson G. Henry as Postmaster at Springfield: "I have, within the last few days, been making a most discreditable exhibition of myself in the way of hypochondriaism and thereby got an impression that Dr. Henry is necessary to my existence. Unless he gets that place he leaves Springfield." A friend described Lincoln as having "two Cat fits and a Duck fit." On January 23, Lincoln wrote Stuart again. "I am now the most miserable man alive. . . . Whether I shall ever be better I can not tell; I awfully forebode I shall not. To remain as

I am is impossible; I must die or be better, it appears to me."

The circumstances under which Mary and Abraham came to marriage nearly two years later number among the oddest in the oddities of courtship. Joshua Fry Speed, perhaps Lincoln's closest friend during this period, had sold his store in Springfield and returned to Kentucky. Lincoln visited Speed in August, 1841, and met Speed's fiancée, Fanny Henning. Like Lincoln, Speed had his uncertainties about marriage, and both men confided their trepidations. As the date set for Speed's marriage, February 15, 1842, approached, Lincoln wrote his friend a reassuring letter, hoping "that your present anxiety and distress about *her* health and *her* life, must and will forever banish those horrid doubts, which I know you sometimes felt, as to the truth of your affection for her." Upon receiving a letter from Speed written the day after his wedding, Lincoln wrote again to clinch his argument.

Springfield, Feb. 25 – 1842 –

Dear Speed:

I received yours of the 12th. written the day you went down to William's place, some days since; but delayed answering it, till I should receive the promised one, of the 16th., which came last night. I opened the latter, with intense anxiety and trepidation – so much, that although it turned out better than I expected, I have hardly yet, at the distance of ten hours, become calm.

I tell you, Speed, our *forebodings,* for which you and I are rather peculiar, are all the worst sort of nonsense. I fancied, from the time I received your letter of *Saturday,* that the one of *Wednesday* was never to come; and yet it *did* come, and what is more, it is perfectly clear, both from its *tone* and *hand-*

Hall of the House of Representatives in the Statehouse.

writing, that you were much *happier,* or, if you think
the term preferable, *less miserable,* when you wrote *it,*
than when you wrote the last one before. You had so
obviously improved, at the very time I so much feared
you would have grown worse. You say that "something
indescribably horrible and alarming still haunts you."
You will not say *that* three months from now, I will
venture. When your nerves once get steady now, the
whole trouble will be over forever. Nor should you
become impatient at their being even very slow, in
becoming steady. Again; you say you much fear that
that Elysium of which you have dreamed so much, is
never to be realized. Well, if it shall not, I dare swear,
it will not be the fault of her who is now your wife.
I now have no doubt that it is the peculiar misfortune
of both you and me, to dream dreams of Elysium far
exceeding all that any thing earthly can realize. Far
short of your dreams as you may be, no woman could
do more to realize them, than that same black eyed
Fanny. If you could but contemplate her through my

45

imagination, it would appear ridiculous to you, that any one should for a moment think of being unhappy with her. My old Father used to have a saying that "If you make a bad bargain, *hug* it the tighter"; and it occurs to me, that if the bargain you have just closed can possibly be called a bad one, it is certainly the most *pleasant one* for applying that maxim to, which my fancy can, by any effort, picture.

I write another letter enclosing this, which you can show her, if she desires it. I do this, because, she would think strangely perhaps should you tell her that you receive no letters from me; or, telling her you do,

Interior of the Stuart-Lincoln law office (Frank Leslie's Illustrated Newspaper, *December 22, 1860*).

should refuse to let her see them.

I close this, entertaining the confident hope, that every successive letter I shall have from you, (which I here pray may not be few, nor far between,) may show you possessing a more steady hand, and cheerful heart, than the last preceding it. As ever, your friend
Lincoln

When a few weeks later Speed wrote that he was "far happier" than he "ever expected to be," Lincoln replied: "I am not going beyond the truth, when I tell you that the short space it took me to read your last letter, gave

me more pleasure, than the total sum of all I have enjoyed since that fatal first of Jany. 41. Since then, it
seems to me, I should been entirely happy, but for the
never-absent idea, that there is *one* still unhappy whom
I have contributed to make so."

During the following summer, Abraham and Mary
began "keeping company" again, more or less secretly at
the home of Simeon Francis, editor of the Springfield
Journal, whose wife was as close a friend of Mary as
Francis was of Lincoln. It may be assumed that more
than literary matters were discussed, but the fact is that
Mary and Abraham began a joint venture into anonymous politics satires, published in the *Journal* during
August and September, comprised of a series of letters
signed "Rebecca," lampooning the very Irish Democrat,
State Auditor James Shields. Only one of these anonymous screeds was actually written by Lincoln, but when
Shields challenged him to a duel for their "slander, vitu-
peration and personal abuse," Lincoln was hard put.
Some of the letters in which Lincoln had no hand were
indeed scurrilous, but at first he could not bring himself
to disavow them. The challenge was tentatively accepted
and a memorandum of specifications of weapons –
"Cavalry broadswords of the largest size" – and an equally
ridiculous set of conditions were drawn up by Lincoln.
In addition, however, Lincoln agreed, upon suggestion
of his second, that Shields might accept an explanation
in lieu of apology, to set forth the facts, and thus the
duel was averted, when Lincoln wrote Shields as follows:

I did write the "Lost Township" letter which appeared in the Journal of the 2nd. Inst. but had no partici-
pation, in any form, in any other article alluding to
you. I wrote that, wholly for political effect. I had no
intention of injuring your personal or private character

or standing as a man or a gentleman; and I did not then think, and do not now think that that article, could produce or has produced that effect against you, and had I anticipated such an effect I would have forborne to write it. And I will add, that your conduct towards me, so far as I knew, had always been gentlemanly; and that I had no personal pique against you, and no cause for any.

Thus brought together, Abraham and Mary were married a few weeks later on November 4, 1842, a fact which Lincoln laconically epitomized in the concluding sentence of a business letter to a lawyer friend: "Nothing new here, except my marrying, which to me, is a matter of profound wonder." The newlyweds took rooms at the Globe Tavern and began a durable, if sometimes tempestuous, marriage. Whatever elements of emotional disturbance in Lincoln's personality may have contributed to his strange courtship, they receded into the depths, and in later years it was Mary who displayed to friends and neighbors flashes of hysteria, jealousy, and uncontrolled rage which prompted some people to give to her the reputation of a shrew, and to Abraham the image of matrimonial martyrdom.

Model of Lincoln's invention, "Improved method of lifting vessels over shoals," whittled by Lincoln and patented 1849.

Lincoln on May 7, 1858.

To Become

Unromantic as it may have seemed to Mary Owens, Lincoln's statement – "I want in all cases to do right" – characterized all his relationships with other people, whether those relationships were of love, close friendship, remote acquaintance, or even those of an adversary with conflicting interests and views. People instinctively trusted him, perhaps, on first looking into his deep, sadly humorous eyes, but only his faithful protection of their trust over months and years made a local legend of his integrity and sympathy long before he became a national figure. Even while he failed completely as a storekeeper in New Salem, he succeeded tremendously in his role as counselor and leader in the frontier community. Politics and the law became thus his inevitable pursuits.

His election within less than a year as captain of the local company of volunteers, albeit the competition was limited, showed him which way the wind blew, and his success in his local precinct, even though he was defeated in his first campaign for a seat in the legislature, fixed the image he envisioned for himself as leader of his folk. This image, to which he would thenceforth devote his life, was sketched at the conclusion of his first published political "Communication to the People of Sangamo County," March 9, 1832: "Every man is said to have his peculiar ambition. Whether it be true or not, I can say for one that I have no other so great as that of being truly esteemed of my fellow men, by rendering myself

51

worthy of their esteem. How far I shall succeed in gratifying this ambition, is yet to be developed."

If politics provided the field of honor, the law was the grindstone to whet the blade. In later years, Lincoln would declare he was "not an accomplished lawyer," but the great majority of his contemporaries at the practice paid him respect as among the best. It is true that his practice was made up chiefly of routine litigation which he characterized as a "great variety of little business," but in it he acquired an intimate knowledge of all manner of human troubles, conflicts, and misunderstandings, which, on however lowly plane, lay at the roots of the epic struggle to which his country was doomed. He learned again and again how, between adversaries, as he phrased it later in the context of the Civil War, "both *may* be, and one *must* be wrong," and as he rode the circuit from courthouse to courthouse down dusty or muddy roads, whether on horseback or as a contemporary remembered him, "behind his own horse, which was an indifferent, raw-boned specimen, in his own

Riding the Eighth Judicial Circuit.

black-smith made buggy – a most ordinary one," he had ample opportunity to reflect and formulate the inimitable phrasing of his thoughts.

2

During the quarter of a century which spanned his life from New Salem to Washington, we have many records of the moments when he was in the public eye, but the increasing stature which they display can be adequately accounted for only by an effort to assess what must have taken place in solitude, thoughtful reading and reflection on the human condition mirrored in the great literary works which from early to late he studied as only a man who wants "in all cases to do right" can study them – the Bible and Shakespeare.

Lincoln knew both the Bible and Shakespeare as well as or better than most clergymen, scholars, or actors in his age, which far more than our own concentrated the education of the literate upon these texts. His prose bears tribute to them, frequently in allusions, but constantly in the poetic rhythm and metaphor, which are often the very matrix of his thought. In addition to these, he was fond of quoting certain minor eighteenth-century poems of the elegiac variety. William Knox's "Mortality" was a favorite, beginning "O why should the spirit of mortal be proud," and Gray's "Elegy" another. When in the fall of 1844 he visited his childhood home in Indiana, he was moved to compose verses which reflect his fondness for these poets, as well as his own emotions, which he was convinced "were certainly poetry; though whether my expression of those feelings is poetry is quite another matter." We may agree that both were poetry, if we assess them by the same standard which made Knox and Gray appeal to Lincoln. Three stanzas of twenty-four will suffice to suggest the whole.

O memory! thou mid-way world
'Twixt Earth and Paradise,
Where things decayed, and loved ones lost
In dreamy shadows rise.

I range the fields with pensive tread,
And pace the hollow rooms,
And feel (companion of the dead)
I'm living in the tombs.

The very spot where grew the bread
That formed my bones I see.
How strange, old field, on thee to tread,
And feel I'm part of thee.

It was the opinion of Herndon, that Lincoln "read less and thought more than any man in his sphere in America," and in describing what seemed to him, as a voracious reader, a painfully slow process, Herndon gave inadvertently the clew to what voracious readers sometimes cannot comprehend – that one takes out no more than he puts in. Lincoln's appreciation of rhythmic language and imagery, as well as his search for understanding in depth, was involved in the process Herndon described. "Mr. Lincoln's habits, methods of reading law, politics, poetry, etc., etc., were to come into the office, pick up book, newspaper, etc., and to sprawl himself out on the sofa chairs, etc., and read aloud, much to my annoyance. I have asked him often why he did so and his invariable reply was: 'I catch the idea by two senses, for when I read aloud I hear what is read and I see it; and hence two senses get it and I remember it better, if I do not understand it better.'"

Yet Herndon was essentially right. Lincoln's study of books, like his study of people and things, was more intense than wide. "Before he could form an idea of anything, before he would express his opinion on any subject, he must know its origin and history in substance and quality, in magnitude and gravity. . . . Thus everything had to run through the crucible, and be tested by the fires of his analytic mind. . . ."

3

Although Lincoln was a profound student of the Bible and was deemed essentially a religious man by those who knew him best, there is no credible record of his profession of a particular faith and allegiance to any denomination of Christianity. After marriage he sometimes attended the Presbyterian Church with his wife, but some of his contemporaries believed him to be an "infidel," and during his compaign for Congress in 1846, supporters of his Democratic opponent, the famous cir-cuit-riding Methodist preacher Peter Cartwright, brought this issue so heavily to bear that Lincoln was compelled to answer by means of a political handbill which stated succinctly what he could say in his own defense.

To the Voters of the Seventh Congressional District.
Fellow Citizens:

A charge having got into circulation in some of the neighborhoods of this District, in substance that I am an open scoffer at Christianity, I have by the advice of some friends concluded to notice the subject in this form. That I am not a member of any Christian Church, is true; but I have never denied the truth of the Scriptures; and I have never spoken with intentional disrespect of religion in general, or any denominational of Christians in particular. It is true that in early life I was inclined to believe in what I understand is called the "Doctrine of Necessity" – that is,

Front parlor in the Lincoln home (Frank Leslie's Illustrated Newspaper, *March 9, 1861*).

that the human mind is impelled to action, or held in rest by some power, over which the mind itself has no control; and I have sometimes (with one, two or three, but never publicly) tried to maintain this opinion in argument. The habit of arguing thus however, I have, entirely left off for more than five years. And I add here, I have always understood this same opinion to be held by several of the Christian denominations. The foregoing, is the whole truth, briefly stated, in relation to myself, upon this subject.

I do not think I could myself, be brought to support a man for office, whom I knew to be an open enemy of, and scoffer at, religion. Leaving the higher matter of eternal consequences, between him and his Maker, I still do not think any man has the right thus to insult the feelings, and injure the morals, of the community in which he may live. If, then, I was guilty of such conduct, I should blame no man who should condemn

me for it; but I do blame those, whoever they may be, who falsely put such a charge in circulation against me.

July 31, 1846.

A. Lincoln.

This statement remains adequate, so far as it goes, in intellectual exposition. Both emotionally and intellectually, however, Lincoln went much beyond this in later life, openly avowing his belief in God and during his Presidency enunciating the simple, fatalistic belief upon which he relied. "The purposes of the almighty are perfect, and must prevail, though we erring mortals may fail to accurately perceive them in advance. We hoped for a happy termination of this terrible war long before this; but God knows best, and has ruled otherwise. We shall yet acknowledge His wisdom and our own error therein. Meanwhile we must work earnestly in the best light He gives us, trusting that so working still conduces to the great ends He ordains."

In essence Lincoln's rational religion, as well as his political philosophy, was not much different from that of Thomas Jefferson, but added to this was a personal strain of mysticism, perhaps verging on superstition, insofar as his own role and ultimate fate were concerned. All the reasoning which he could bring to bear merely corroborated his conviction that he and the events through which he passed were controlled by a power which had a design for ultimate fulfillment. It was this which gave him a conviction of destiny to be fulfilled, like the heroes in his favorite Shakespearean plays.

4

Lincoln's campaign against Peter Cartwright was largely won before it began, as a result of careful strategy in keeping the Whigs unified in their central Illinois stronghold, the Seventh Congressional District which embraced Springfield and the Sangamon area where Lincoln was an acknowledged leader. Keeping Whigs unified was more difficult in some respects than defeating Democrats, since the Whigs were highly individualistic in their party politics. Against Lincoln's consistent recommendations they long refused to adopt the county and state convention system which had proved so successful in keeping the Democrats together, and even after they had adopted it, many Whigs refused to be bound by the nominations made in convention, and announced candidacies on their own hook, running against their party's nominees as well as against the nominated Democrats.

Lincoln's two rival Whig leaders in the Seventh District were John. J. Hardin of Morgan County and Edward D. Baker, like Lincoln a resident of Sangamon. At this stage in their respective careers, Hardin was the better trained and more successful lawyer, having graduated from Transylvania University and studied law under Chief Justice John Boyle of the Kentucky court of appeals. Baker, an English immigrant, was like Lincoln largely self-taught, but mixed his law practice and politics with preaching in the Campbellite churches of the region. He was credited with being the ablest extemporaneous speaker in Illinois and when he went to Congress won the compliments of ex-President John Quincy Adams for his eloquent speeches. With such competition, Lincoln's strategy in 1842 was to negotiate an "understanding" that each of the three should take a turn as Whig candidate for Congress, with Baker following Hardin and Lincoln following Baker. When Lincoln's turn came in 1846, there was considerable argument about whether such an understanding had been agreed to in hard and fast terms; nevertheless Lincoln received the nomination and handily won the election over Cartwright.

Lincoln's record in Congress appears greater in historical retrospect, as a step in his larger career, than it appeared at the time, chiefly perhaps because his one major speech in Congress, "The War with Mexico," delivered on January 12, 1848, marked a new level in Lincoln's political thought and expression. However effective it may appear in retrospect, it won him no support at home and required much defense against his opponents' popular, patriotic espousal of the Mexican War as a just cause. When his law partner William H. Herndon wrote him a warning letter to the effect that his course of action in censuring President Polk for beginning the war (the official Whig line) was something less than popular, his defense was that when "compelled to speak . . . your only alternative is to tell the *truth* or tell a *lie*." when he summarized his position on this subject in his autobiographical sketch written following his nomination for the presidency in 1860, he took care to define, if not to apologize for, this principal political "error" of his early career, as follows:

All the battles of the Mexican war had been fought before Mr. Lincoln took his seat in Congress, but the American army was still in Mexico, and the treaty of peace was not fully and formally ratified till the June afterwards. Much has been said of his course in Congress in regard to this war. A careful examination of the Journals and Congressional Globe shows, that he voted for all the supply measures which came up, and for all the measures in any way favorable to the officers, soldiers, and their families, who conducted the war through; with this exception that some of these measures passed without yeas and nays, leaving no record as to how particular men voted. The Journals

Lincoln and his sons William Wallace and Thomas (Tad) standing in their front yard, January, 1861.

and Globe also show him voting that the war was unnecessarily and unconstitutionally begun by the President of the United States. This is the language of Mr. [George] Ashmun's amendment, for which Mr. Lincoln and nearly or quite all, other Whigs of the House of Representatives voted.

Mr. Lincoln's reasons for the opinion expressed by this vote were briefly that the President had sent General Taylor into an inhabited part of the country belonging to Mexico, and not to the U.S. and thereby had provoked the first act of hostility – in fact the commencement of the war; that the place, being the country bordering on the East bank of the Rio Grande, was inhabited by native Mexicans, born there under the Mexican government; and had never submitted to, nor been conquered by Texas, or the U.S., nor transferred to either by treaty – that although Texas claimed the Rio Grande as her boundary, Mexico had never recognized it, and neither Texas nor the U.S. had ever enforced it – that there was a broad desert between that, and the country over which Texas had actual control – that the country where hostilities commenced, having once belonged to Mexico, must remain so, until it was somehow legally transferred, which had never been done.

Mr. Lincoln thought the act of sending an armed force among the Mexicans, was *unnecessary,* inasmuch as Mexico was in no way molesting, or menacing the U.S. or the people thereof; and that it was *unconstitutional*, because the power of levying war is vested in Congress, and not in the President. He thought the principal motive for the act, was to divert public attention from the surrender of "Fifty-four, forty, or fight" to Great Britain, on the Oregon boundary question.

It was just as well that Lincoln had no intention of running for re-election, for in all probability he would have been as soundly beaten as was his former law partner Stephen T. Logan, whose turn it was to run. Nevertheless, the popularity of the Whig candidate for the presidency in 1848, the Hero of Buena Vista, General Zachary Taylor, was such that he carried Lincoln's district by a majority of something over 1,500 votes. Lincoln had been one of the earliest advocates of and hardest fighters for Taylors nomination, "in opposition to all others," and following the nomination took an active part in the successful campaign for Taylor's election, speaking in Maryland and Massachusetts as well as in Illinois.

During the months between Taylor's election in November and his inauguration in March, Lincoln carried on efforts to obtain a post in the cabinet for his old friend and predecessor Colonel Edward D. Baker, who had distinguished himself heroically in the Mexican War and returned to be elected as the only Whig Representative from Illinois, this time from the Sixth District in the northwestern part of the state. This, as well as many of Lincoln's other efforts to obtain lesser appointments for worthy Illinois Whigs, who like Lincoln had been early Taylor men, came to naught. Likewise, he had no success with the one important measure he tried to introduce in the House of Representatives, a bill providing for the abolition of slavery in the District of Columbia. When he returned to Springfield after the inauguration, he continued his efforts without success to obtain appointment to the General Land Office, either for an Illinois Whig whom he would recommend, or for himself. Finally, late in August, he was offered appointment as Secretary of the Territory of Oregon, when he had hoped to be appointed Governor. He "respectfully" declined, and when a few weeks later he was offered the appointment as Governor, he declined that also. Nothing could have made his lack of weight with the new administration more humiliatingly apparent, but added to the obviousness of his own political eclipse was the spectacle of disintegration going on within the Whig Party itself, to some extent the result of bumbling inadequacy on the part of the Hero of Buena Vista, whom Lincoln had so early advocated as his party's candidate for President of the United States.

With good reason, Lincoln returned chastened to his practice of law, as he said, "with greater earnestness than ever before," and for the next five years his profession "almost superseded the thought of politics."

5

Whatever his sense of destiny may have been during the years 1849-1854, it is not discoverable in the letters, speeches, or legal documents which record his routine activities at this time. Upon completing his term in Congress, he remained without a discernible purpose in politics beyond keeping in touch with his disintegrating Whig Party, which itself had become largely without purpose other than to try to stay on the gravy train of political patronage by electing another military hero. Having succeeded with General Zachary Taylor in 1848, why not again in 1852 with General Winfield Scott? Although opposed to slavery in principle, Lincoln like most other Whigs was willing to let well enough alone. Not so the Democrats, however, with the balance of power within their party shifting heavily to the slave states.

With the defeat of Scott by Franklin Pierce, a New Hampshire Democrat amenable to the slave state interests, the Whig Party finally disintegrated and the Democratic Party obtained an apparently sweeping control of national politics. Within the Democratic

Party, however, there was danger of a split. The northern Democrats, albeit generally amenable to limited extension of slavery into the territories, were not wholly pleased with the growing arrogance and presumption of the slavery extremists of the party, who insistently thrust the question of slavery extension into party caucus and, in the form of various bills, into the House of Representatives and the Senate.

In this intra-party strife it became the role of Lincoln's great adversary, Stephen A. Douglas, to work out a formula acceptable to both wings of his party, and he hoped to the nation as a whole. Thus "Popular Sovereignty" became the formula on which it was hoped the Democrats could more or less agree as the best means of keeping both wings together, and which in fact enabled the party to keep control of the Senate from 1852 to 1860. Popular Sovereignty meant that the people of any territory should have the right to decide by popular vote, at the time the territory was admitted into the Union, whether it would be admitted as a slave state or a free state. It was put into practice in 1854 in Section 14 of the bill to admit Kansas into the Union – the so-called Kansas-Nebraska law, which divided the Nebraska Territory and provided for the repeal of the Missouri Compromise of 1820, which had excluded slavery from the Nebraska Territory while admitting Missouri as a slave state. The Kansas-Nebraska law stated that this exclusion of slavery was "inconsistent with the principles of non-intervention by congress with slavery in the State and Territories as recognized by the legislation of eighteen hundred and fifty, commonly called the compromise measures . . . it being the true intent and meaning of this act not to legislate slavery into any territory or State, nor to exclude it therefrom, but to leave the people thereof perfectly free to form and regulate their domestic

Sitting room in the Lincoln home (Frank Leslie's Illustrated Newspaper, March 9, 1861).

institutions in their own way. . . ." In brief, where the Missouri Compromise had excluded slavery, the Kansas-Nebraska bill opened the territories to slavery. The double talk about not meaning to legislate slavery into the territories meant only, as Lincoln phrased it, "that it does not require slaves to be sent there."

This was the event which brought Lincoln actively back into politics, and which ultimately was responsible for his election to the presidency after six years of continual and unremitting attack upon the workings of Popular Sovereignty. It was likewise the event which brought about an almost spontaneous coalescence of anti-slavery men – whether Whigs, Democrats, Free-Soilers, or Know-Nothings – into the new Republican Party. Although these "fusion" meetings throughout 1854-55 took place in all northern states, the name "Republican" was first adopted on July 6, 1854, by a mass meeting at Jackson, Michigan.

Lincoln was by no means alone among Illinoisans opposed to Popular Sovereignty and rapidly became their leader following the delivery of his history-making speech "The Repeal of the Missouri Compromise and the Pro-

priety of Its Restoration," which although delivered in
part in various Illinois towns during August, and in its
entirety at Springfield on October 4, became known as the
"Peoria Speech" following its delivery there on October
16, 1854. It was printed in full in the *Illinois Journal*
and became the most widely noticed pronouncement
Lincoln had made up to this time. More than seventeen
thousand words in length, it presented a masterly analysis
of the history of legislation on slavery extension from
the Ordinance of 1787 and the Louisiana Purchase in
1803 to the passage of the Kansas-Nebraska bill. Its
climax was a clarion that called all Americans to readopt
the Declaration of Independence in order to preserve
their own liberty.

Fellow countrymen – Americans south, as well as
north, shall we make no effort to arrest this? Already
the liberal party throughout the world, express the
apprehension "that the one retrograde institution in
America, is undermining the principles of progress,
and fatally violating the noblest political system the

world ever saw." This is not the taunt of enemies, but the warning of friends. Is it quite safe to disregard it – to despise it? Is there no danger to liberty itself, in discarding the earliest practice, and first precept of our ancient faith? In our greedy chase to make profit of the negro, let us beware, lest we "cancel and tear to pieces" even the white man's charter of freedom.

Our republican robe is soiled, and trailed in the dust. Let us repurify it. Let us turn and wash it white, in the spirit, if not the blood, of the Revolution. Let us turn slavery from its claims of "moral right," back upon its existing legal rights, and its arguments of "necessity." Let us return it to the position our fathers gave it; and there let it rest in peace. Let us re-adopt the Declaration of Independence, and with it, the practices, and policy, which harmonize with it. Let north and south – let all Americans – let all lovers of liberty everywhere – join in the great and good work. If we do this, we shall not only have saved the Union; but we shall have so saved it, as to make, and to keep it, forever worthy of the saving. We shall have so saved it, that the succeeding millions of free happy people, the world over, shall rise up, and call us blessed, to the latest generations.

In his reluctance to abandon the Whig Party, however, Lincoln at first avoided identification with the Republicans, preferring to be known merely as "an Anti-Nebraska man," in his first campaign for U.S. Senator during the winter of 1854-1855. When the Illinois legislature met in February to elect the new Senator, the Anti-Nebraska members held a majority of thirteen – Whigs, Democrats, and a few newly elected Republicans. On the first ballot Lincoln received 44 votes, James A. Shields 41, and Lincoln's old friend Lyman Trumbull 5, with a scattering of other votes. But on succeeding ballots it became apparent that not Shields but Governor Joel Matteson, a purported Anti-Nebraska Democrat, was the real opposition, and when several of Lincoln's original supporters began to defect, Lincoln threw his support to Trumbull in order to guarantee that the Senator-elect would represent the genuine Anti-Nebraska feeling in Illinois.

Lincoln wrote to his friend Elihu Washburne the next day, "I regret me defeat moderately, but I am not nervous about it. I could have headed off every combination and been elected, had it not been for Matteson's double game – and his defeat gives me more pleasure than my own gives me pain. On the whole, it is perhaps as well for our general cause that Trumbull is elected. The Neb. men confess that they hate it worse than any thing that could have happened. It is a great consolation to see them worse whipped than I am."

6

Following his defeat Lincoln returned to his law practice, as he said in a letter to Republican Owen Lovejoy, in order "to pick up my lost crumbs of last year." He was just as anxious as Lovejoy to prevent the extension of slavery "and yet the political atmosphere is such, just now, that I fear to do any thing, lest I do wrong." He was afraid particularly of the element of Know-Nothingism in the opposition to slavery extension. "I have no objection to "fuse" with any body provided I can fuse on ground which I think is right; and I believe the opponents of slavery extension could now do this if it were not for the K. N. ism." Likewise in a letter to his old friend Joshua Speed, Lincoln expressed his fear of the Know-Nothings: "How can any one who abhors the oppression of negroes, be in favor of degrading classes of white people? Our progress in degeneracy appears to me to be pretty rapid. As a nation, we began by declaring that *'all men are created equal.'* We now practically read it 'all men are created equal, *except negroes.'* When the Know-Nothings get control, it will read 'all men are created equal, except negroes, *and foreigners, and Catholics.'* When it comes to this I should prefer emigrating to some country where they make no pretense of loving liberty – to Russia, for instance, where despotism can be taken pure, and without the base alloy of hypocrisy."

Meanwhile, Kansas was rapidly becoming a battleground of the forces which would ultimately erupt in the Civil War. Societies which had been formed in Massachusetts and other northern states even before the territory had been opened for settlement were promoting the

$1200 TO 1250 DOLLARS! FOR NEGROES!!

THE undersigned wishes to purchase a large lot of NEGROES for the New Orleans market. I will pay $1200 to $1250 for No. 1 young men, and $850 to $1000 for No. 1 young women. In fact I will pay more for likely

NEGROES,

Than any other trader in Kentucky. My office is adjoining the Broadway Hotel, on Broadway, Lexington, Ky., where I or my Agent can always be found.

WM. F. TALBOTT.

LEXINGTON, JULY 2, 1853.

69

Handbill advertising for slaves.

emigration of antislavery settlers, and slavery interests, particularly in adjacent Missouri, were encouraging slave-holders to emigrate. Although Kansas had from the beginning more proslavery than free-soil settlers, in the November, 1854 election of a territorial delegate to Congress, additional hundreds of Missourians crossed the border merely for the purpose of electing the proslavery candidate. In March, 1855 the Missourians again moved in to elect the territorial legislature, this time with guns. Later investigation proved that more than two-third of the votes cast were fraudulent. In May, 1854 the predominantly antislavery town of Lawrence was sacked by proslavery forces and free-soil forces prompty retaliated. Particularly famous was the raid by John Brown and a party of six, including four of his sons, who massacred five proslavery victims. The territory was popularly referred to with some justice as "Bleeding Kansas."

Lincoln's forecast had proved accurate. He had written Speed in August, 1855: "That Kansas will form a Slave Constitution, and, with it, will ask to be admitted into the Union, I take to be an already settled question." But by the time the question came before Congress, anti-slavery forces were in the ascendant, and the admission of Kansas under the Lecompton Constitution was voted down.

By May, 1856 Lincoln had made up his mind to "fuse" with other antislavery men, and at the Republican state convention on May 26 delivered a speech calculated to weld the diffuse elements of the new party on the principle that the "Union must be preserved in the purity of its principles as well as in the integrity of its territorial parts." Although this speech became legendary as one of Lincoln's highest oratorical flights, it was not recorded except for a few sentences, including the phrase just quoted, as reported in the Alton *Weekly Courier,* June 5,

1856. Two years before, Lincoln had been scarcely known outside of Illinois, but when the first national convention of the Republican Party met in Philadelphia on June 17 to nominate General John C. Frémont and William L. Dayton as candidates for President and Vice-President, Lincoln ran second on the nomination for Vice-President with 110 votes.

Following the Republican national convention, Lincoln took the stump to make over fifty speeches, the gist of all being the necessity that the electorate recognize the one important issue before them. He said: "It is constantly objected to Frémont and Dayton that they are supported by a *sectional* party, who by their *sectionalism,* endanger the National Union." But, he continued, the question between the two parties was simply " 'Shall slavery be allowed to extend into U.S. territories, now legally free?' Buchanan says it *shall;* and Frémont says it shall *not.* That is the *naked* issue, and the *whole* of it. . . . I beg to know *how one* side of that question is more sectional than the other? . . . It is not because one *side* of the question dividing them, is more sectional than the *other;* nor because of any difference, in the mental or moral structure of the people North and South. It is because, in that question, the people of the South have an immediate palpable and immensely great pecuniary interest; while, with the people of the North, it is merely an abstract question of moral right, with only *slight,* and *remote* pecuniary interest added. . . . This *is* the sectional question – that is to say, it is a question, in its nature calculated to divide the American people geographically. Who is to *blame* for that? *Who* can help it? Either side can help it; but how? Simply by yielding to the other side. There is no other way. Then, which side shall yield? To this again, there can be but one answer – the side which is *wrong.* True, we differ, as to which side *is* wrong; and we boldly say, let all who really think slavery ought to spread into free territory, openly go over against us.... But why should any go, who really think slavery ought not to spread? Do they think that *right* ought to yield to *wrong*?"

Although the Republicans lost the election, they had

Lincoln's advice to a student: letter to Isham Reavis.

the issue as phrased by Lincoln, upon which they would continue to campaign for the next four years, and on which Lincoln would be elected as James Buchanan's successor to the Presidency of the United States.

7

In 1857 came the Dred Scott Decision, which declared the Missouri Compromise unconstitutional; Congress could not prohibit slavery in the territories. Hence, what Lincoln and all Republicans were advocating was, according to the Supreme Court, against the Constitution itself. Made by a divided Court, the decision was, Lincoln held, erroneous and subject to being overruled by the Court in a later decision. "We know the court that made it, has often overruled its own decisions, and we shall do what we can to have it overrule this. We offer no *resistance* to it."

In simple, human terms, Lincoln undertook to define the difference between Republican and Democratic positions as represented not merely in the division in party politics but also in the divided Court. "The Republicans inculcate, with whatever ability they can, that the Negro is a man, that his bondage is cruelly wrong, and that the field of his oppression ought not to be enlarged. The Democrats deny his manhood; deny or dwarf to insignificance, the wrong of his bondage; so far as possible, crush all sympathy for him, and cultivate and excite hatred and disgust against him; complimenting themselves as Union-servers for doing so; and call the indefinite outspreading of his bondage 'a sacred right of self-government.'"

In June, 1858, Lincoln accepted the nomination of the Republican State Convention as candidate for U.S. Senator against Stephen A. Douglas. Now all other issues had become lost in the overwhelming concern for and against slavery extension. In his acceptance speech Lincoln defined the political trend in biting rhetoric:

> If we could first know *where* we are, and *whither* we are tending, we could then better judge *what* to do, and *how* to do it.
>
> We are now far into the *fifth* year, since a policy was initiated, with the *avowed* object, and *confident* promise, of putting an end to slavery agitation.
>
> Under the operation of that policy, that agitation has not only, *not ceased*, but has *constantly augmented*.
>
> In *my* opinion, it *will* not cease, until a *crisis* shall have been reached, and passed.
>
> "A house divided against itself cannot stand."
>
> I believe this government cannot endure, permanently half *slave* and half *free*.
>
> I do not expect the Union to be *dissolved* – I do not expect the house to *fall* – but I *do* expect it will cease to be divided.
>
> It will become *all* one thing, or *all* the other.
>
> Either the *opponents* of slavery, will arrest the further spread of it, and place it where the public mind shall rest in the belief that it is in course of ultimate extinction; or its *advocates* will push it forward, till it shall become alike lawful in *all* the States, *old* as well as *new* – *North* as well as *South*.

The campaign that followed was perhaps the most strenuous ever conducted in American politics up to that time. Douglas was the acknowledged leader of his party not merely in Illinois but for the majority of Democrats in the northern and border states as well. He fully appreciated the intellectual capacity and political effectiveness of his antagonist. During June and July he found it impossible to avoid the issue or the man and met Lincoln's unremitting attack head on, using every art known to him to defend his formula of Popular Sovereignty and to counterattack with the general theme of the identity of "Nigger-loving" and "Black Republicanism."

On July 24 Lincoln challenged Douglas to a series of joint debates. It has often been pointed out that Douglas as the established figure displayed great magnanimity in accepting the challenge of a Johnny-come-lately Lincoln. While not detracting from any possible magnanimity on the part of Douglas, the fact cannot be dismissed that Douglas expected to gain more for the immediate election by accepting the challenge than he would lose by rejecting it. A hero cannot continue to evade an adversary who is pressing the fight. The debates which ensued marked the great turning point in Lincoln's career, in spite of the fact that they failed to prove Lincoln's unquestioned superiority as a debater or to bring about his election to replace Douglas in the Senate. Their real effect was to bring Lincoln sharply to the forefront on the national scene, and to furnish the essential text upon which he would be nominated and elected President two years later in a campaign conducted wholly without speechmaking by a candidate whose qualities as a speechmaker were by that time pre-eminent.

The dramatic elements in the struggle between Douglas and Lincoln were not confined to differences in political philosophy or to their apparently equal intellectual and rhetorical abilities. Their contrasts were sharp on every plane. "The Little Giant" stood five feet tall against Lincoln's six feet four inches. Where Lincoln appeared gangling and awkward, drolly humorous and smolderingly sarcastic by turns, Douglas appeared well kept and sturdy, emanating a boundless energy and a sharp, quick wit and sarcasm that cut to the bone. Where Lincoln presented an image of integrity at the expense of success,

Douglas presented an image of successful expediency, not necessarily without integrity but suspected of compromising ultimate ends for temporarily successful means to power. Each man made, to the best of his ability, the most of his assets and turned his liabilities wherever he could into assets. So Douglas plucked the string that all his thoughts and acts were motivated by the desire to preserve the Union, and Lincoln stressed the double intent of preserving the Union and preserving as well the Declaration of Independence as its basic truth.

Lincoln concluded the campaign on this note:

I have said that in some respects the contest has

Stephen A. Douglas.

been painful to me. Myself, and those with whom I act have been constantly accused of a purpose to destroy the union; and bespattered with every imaginable odious epithet; and some who were friends, as it were but yesterday have made themselves most active in this. I have cultivated patience, and made no attempt at a retort.

Ambition has been ascribed to me. God knows how sincerely I prayed from the first that this field of ambition might not be opened. I claim no insensibility to political honors; but today could the Missouri restriction be restored, and the whole slavery

Lincoln.

question replaced on the old ground of "toleration" by *necessity* where it exists, with unyielding hostility to the spread of it, on principle, I would, in consideration, gladly agree, that Judge Douglas should never be *out,* and I never *in,* an office, so long as we both or either, live.

8

Although Lincoln defeated Douglas by a popular plurality of some 4,000 votes, when the legislature met to cast the decisive vote the existing apportionment of the legislature in favor of the southern districts of Illinois gave Douglas 54 votes to Lincoln's 46. Far from being dispirited, Lincoln began almost immediately to reassure the disconsolate. On November 15, he wrote his campaign manager, Norman B. Judd, that "the fight must go on," and on the day following wrote again about campaign expenses, "I am willing to pay according to my ability, but I am the poorest hand to get others to pay. I have been on expenses so long without earning any thing that I am absolutely without money even for household purposes. Still, if you can put in two hundred and fifty dollars . . . I will allow it when you and I settle . . . [and] will exceed my subscription of five hundred dollars . . . exclusive of my ordinary expenses during the campaign. . . . You are feeling badly. *'And this too shall pass away.'* Never fear." To his old friend Anson G. Henry he wrote, "I am glad I made the race. It gave me a hearing on the great and durable question of the age. . . . I believe I have made some marks which will tell for the cause of civil liberty long after I am gone."

Lincoln's "marks" in the Great Debates were far from the peak of his ascent; during the next year and a half he carved out a series of rising notches on the cliff of public opinion, writing public letters, lecturing, and delivering political addresses from Kansas to New York and New England. Unable to accept an invitation to address a Boston audience in honor of Jefferson's birthday, on April 13, 1859, he sent a letter to be read which concluded, "All honor to Jefferson – to the man who, in the concrete pressure of a struggle for national independence by a single people, had the coolness, forecast, and capacity to introduce into a merely revolutionary document, an abstract truth, applicable to all men and all times . . . a rebuke and a stumbling block to the very harbingers of re-appearing tyranny and oppression."

At Cincinnati on September 17, he spoke to an audience with a large representation of Kentuckians from across the Ohio river: "You are trying to show that slavery existed in Bible times by Divine ordinance. Now Douglas is wiser than you, for your own benefit, upon that subject. Douglas knows that whenever you establish that Slavery was right by the Bible, it will occur that that Slavery was the Slavery of the *white* man – of men without reference to color – and he knows very well that you may entertain that idea in Kentucky as much as you please, but you will never win any Northern support for it." He continued his observations on free versus slave labor with a personal allusion. "We know, Southern men declare that their slaves are better off than hired laborers amongst us. How little they know, whereof they speak! There is no permanent class of hired laborers amongst us. Twenty-five years ago, I was a hired laborer."

At Beloit, Wisconsin, on September 30, he spoke to an audience at an agricultural fair, elaborating his economic tenet of equal opportunitiy for all in opposition to the "mud-sill" theory that a fixed labor force is necessary to civilization, with the statement that "labor is prior to, and independent of, capital; that, in fact, capital is the

Lincoln at Cooper Institute, February 27, 1860.

fruit of labor, and could never have existed if labor had not *first* existed – that labor can exist without capital, but that capital could never have existed without labor." The error of the "mud-sill" theory, he pointed out, was in assuming "that the *whole* labor of the world exists within that relation" in which "labor is available only in connection with capital." He continued, tying together the country's needs for labor and for education and pointing out that according to the "mud-sill" theory "the education of laborers, is not only useless, but pernicious and dangerous. . . . But Free Labor says 'no!' Free Labor argues that as the Author of man makes every individual with one head and one pair of hands, it was probably intended that heads and hands should co-operate as friends; and that that particular head, should direct and control that particular pair of hands. . . . In one word Free Labor insists on universal education."

At Cooper Institute in New York City on February 27, 1860, he addressed a critical and sophisticated audience which numbered many of the leading figures of the eastern wing of the Republican party. This address went far toward clinching the support of eastern newspaper editors like William Cullen Bryant and Horace Greeley, the latter motivated in his quest for a candidate by a powerful determination to prevent the choice of Senator William H. Seward of New York in the forthcoming national convention in June. Taking as his text Senator Douglas' contention that "Our fathers, when they framed the Government under which we live, understood this question [slavery extension] just as well, and even better, than we do now," Lincoln gave a masterly historical dissertation on the records of the framing of the Constitution, the adoption of the Ordinance of 1787, and the passage of the Missouri Compromise, to expose Douglas' error in implying that the Fathers believed "proper division of local from federal authority ... forbade the Federal Government to control as to slavery in the federal territories.... Let all who believe that 'our

Where Lincoln was nominated (Harper's Weekly, *May 12, 1860).*

fathers ... understood this question'... speak as they spoke, and act as they acted upon it. This is all Republicans ask – all Republicans desire – in relation to slavery..... Neither let us be slandered from our duty by false accusations against us, nor frightened from it by menaces of destruction to the Government nor of dungeons to ourselves. Let us have faith that right makes might, and in that faith, let us, to the end, dare to do our duty as we understand it."

9

On May 9 and 10, 1860, the Illinois state Republican convention met at Decatur in Macon County, completely controlled by Lincoln's adherents. It was an ovation rather than a convention, and contributed the symbol which would represent Lincoln's advocacy of free labor and equal opportunity in simplest and most palpable personal terms. Farmer John Hanks, who had accompanied

the Lincoln trek from Indiana to Macon County, Illinois in 1830, strode down the aisle, assisted by a friend, carrying a banner on two fence rails:

ABRAHAM LINCOLN

The Rail Candidate for President
in 1860

In smaller letters, the legend continued, "Two Rails from a lot of 3,000 Made in 1830 by Thos. Hanks and Abe Lincoln – Whose Father was the First Pioneer of Macon County." There ensued a typically frenzied convention demonstration after which Lincoln acknowledged that although he could not be sure he had made those particular rails, he had certainly split better ones. Thus Lincoln became for the duration of the campaign the "Rail-Splitter" candidate, and afterwards throughout his presidency the "Rail-Splitter" President.

When the Republican national convention met in the Wigwam at Chicago in June, the going was tougher, but Lincoln's exceedingly well organized Illinois forces, led by his old friend Judge David Davis, combined with supporters from Indiana and the New England states in particular, as well as with the personal efforts of Horace Greeley who had been excluded from a seat on the New York delegation by Seward's followers, to give Lincoln 102 votes to Seward's 173½ on the first ballot. On the second ballot Lincoln gained 79 votes while Seward gained only 11, and on the third ballot Lincoln held 231½ to Seward's 180, only 1½ votes short of the nomination. In a matter of minutes a change of 4 votes in the Ohio delegation gave Lincoln the nomination.

Lincoln was in the office of the *Illinois State Journal* with friends when the news came over the wires. He is reputed to have said, "There is a little lady down the

street who would like to know something about this."
Whereupon he went home to tell her. Mary Todd Lincoln had been known to have expressed on more than
one occasion her belief that "Mr. Lincoln" would one day
be President, and this was her first earnest money on
what must have seemed, at times, a very long bet indeed.
During the nearly twenty years that had elapsed since
"that fatal first of Jany. '41," she had had her share of
trials and disappointments – a husband who was sometimes more away from home than he was in it, and when
at home preoccupied, not neglectful perhaps but often
unable to communicate or to carry a husband's fair share

Lincoln in defeat: letter to Henry Asbury.

The convention in session (Harper's Weekly, *May 19, 1860).*

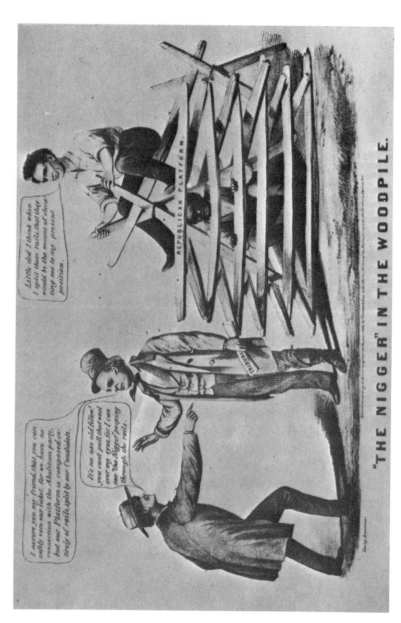

of familial duties. In the ensuing weeks, she adapted her home with consummate grace to the endless chain of callers, one of whom, a reporter from the New York *Evening Post*, paid her the kind of compliment she could appreciate: "She is quite a pattern of ladylike courtesy and polish."

10

While the Republican Party had been fusing all the more solidly, the Democratic Party had split in two. The Northern delegates nominated Douglas as expected, but the disaffected Southern wing nominated John Breckenridge of Kentucky. A new party called the Constitutional Union Party nominated John Bell of Tennessee. As a result, in the November election Lincoln won every Northern state and California and Oregon as well. Breckenridge won the Southern states, excepting Virginia and Tennessee but including Delaware and Maryland, and Douglas and Bell divided the remainder between them. Thus Lincoln became President with less than a majority of the popular vote and was confronted with the problem of trying to get the South to accept him until he could demonstrate that he bore no ill will and would deal fairly with them, within the bounds of his commitment against the further extension of slavery. In order to avoid further inflaming the South he had made no campaign speeches. Similarly, following his election, he avoided public statement. To his old Whig colleague during his term in Congress, Alexander H. Stephens, he wrote a letter marked "For your eye only," expressing his concern: "Do the people of the South really entertain fears that a Republican administration would, *directly* or *indirectly*, interfere with their slaves, or with them, about their slaves? If they do, I wish to assure you, as once a friend, and still, I hope, not an enemy, that there is no

Campaign cartoon (Currier & Ives, 1860).

THE COMING MAN'S PRESIDENTIAL CAREER, à la BLONDIN.

Campaign cartoon (Harper's Weekly, *August 25, 1860*).

cause for such fears." But to no avail. From his election to his inauguration he had to watch the Union gradually dissolve, while the Buchanan administration did nothing to prevent it. On February 11, 1861, the day before his birthday, Lincoln stood on the platform of the train that was taking him to Washington and spoke from his heart to assembled friends and neighbors:

My friends – No one, not in my situation, can appreciate my feeling of sadness at this parting. To this place, and the kindness of these people, I owe every thing. Here I have lived a quarter of a century, and passed from a young to an old man. Here my children have been born, and one is buried. I now leave, not knowing when, or whether ever, I may return, with a task before me greater than that which rested upon Washington. Without the assistance of that Divine Being, who ever attended him, I cannot succeed. With that assistance I cannot fail. Trusting in Him, who can go with me, and remain with you and be every where for good, let us confidently hope that all will yet be well. To His care commending you, as I hope in your prayers you will commend me, I bid you an affectionate farewell.

Lincoln in February, 1861.

The Lineaments of Greatness

If Lincoln had remained silent too long, as some felt, he now began one of the most intensive short campaigns in American history. From February 11, the day he left Springfield, to February 23, the day he arrived in Washington, he made no fewer than seventy-five speeches along the railroad route selected to take him to the capital. Some comprised only a few impromptu sentences, others were longer, and some carefully written down in advance; taken altogether they displayed Lincoln's best talents in an attempt to persuade the people, North and South alike, to give him a chance. In a special appeal to the Kentuckians in his audience at Cincinnati, and beyond them to citizens throughout the South, he promised, "We mean to treat you, as near as we possibly can, as Washington, Jefferson, and Madison treated you. We mean to leave you alone. . . . We mean to remember you are as good as we; that there is no difference between us, other than the difference of circumstance. . . ." But such remarks did not reach the average citizen of the South, for the simple reason that the newspapers of the South were closed to Lincoln, as they had been largely closed to Republican expressions for a period of more than two years. One of the greatest failures in American history, of a supposedly free press nevertheless closely controlled by partisan and economic interests, was the failure of Southern newspapers to give Lincoln a hearing before the people of the South. While there was a Democratic press throughout the North which presented, not equally perhaps, but nevertheless adequately, the arguments of the Breckenridge wing as well as those of the Douglas wing of the Democratic party, there was no medium of communication in the South which would permit the citizen to hear both sides and judge for himself.

Not all of Lincoln's whistle-stop remarks were confined to serious politics. At Westfield, New York, he was reminded that "Some three months ago, I received a letter from a young lady here; it was a very pretty letter, and she advised me to let my whiskers grow, as it would improve my personal appearance; acting partly on her suggestion I have done so; and now, if she is here, I would like to see her. . . ." Whereupon Grace Bedell, age twelve, was pointed out, and Lincoln walked through the crowd and gave her "several hearty kisses amid yells of delight."

At Philadelphia Lincoln received warning of a plot to assassinate him, but the audience assembled to hear him at Independence Hall was unaware of any special cause for the personal allusion in his moving tribute to the Declaration of Independence, "giving liberty not alone to the people of this country, but hope to the world for all future time. . . . I would rather be assassinated on this spot than to surrender it." Although the unfriendly press was quick to ridicule him when a few nights later, on good advice, he slipped quietly from Philadelphia into Washington through the rioting city of Baltimore, few seemed much concerned with the pathos of a nation whose President-elect was reduced to such a stratagem. The rumor that he had been disguised in a long cloak and Scotch-plaid cap provided a field day for cartoonists. Whatever dignity the Presidency might again attain began that night in the humiliation which Lincoln was obliged to accept in order to preserve, not himself alone, but the nation he would rededicate two and a half years later, in

IE NEW PRESIDENT OF THE UNITED STATES
FROM A FUGITIVE SKETCH.

another Pennsylvania town, to "government of the people, by the people, for the people."

2

On March 4, Lincoln delivered his Inaugural Address on the steps of an unfinished Capitol which symbolized a hope that might never be achieved. The crowd numbered a large portion of the indifferent and the disaffected. Washington itself was more Southern in its sympathies than were many communities even in the neighboring states of Maryland and Virginia, as well as in border slave states Kentucky and Missouri. To those assembled and to all citizens whose newspapers would print his words, Lincoln reviewed with utmost pains the limited, conservative position which he had adopted nearly nine years before at Peoria, and had maintained consist-

95

ently in all his speeches since then. "I do but quote from one of those speeches when I declare that 'I have no purpose, directly or indirectly, to interfere with the institution of slavery in the States where it exists. I believe I have no lawful right to do so, and I have no inclination to do so.'" But there could be no doubt, "I hold, that in contemplation of universal law, and of the Constitution, the Union of these States is perpetual. . . . I therefore consider that, in view of the Constitution and the laws, the Union is unbroken; and, to the extent of my ability, I shall take care, as the Constitution expressly enjoins upon me, that the laws of the Union be faithfully executed in all the States. . . . Physically speaking we cannot separate, . . . Can aliens make treaties easier than friends can make laws? . . . Suppose you go to war, you cannot fight always; and when after much loss on both sides, and no gain on either, you cease fighting, the identical old questions, as to terms of intercourse, are again upon you. . . . This country, with its institutions, belongs to the people who inhabit it. . . . Why should there not be a patient confidence in the ultimate justice of the people? . . . I am loth to close. We are not enemies, but friends. We must not be enemies. Though passion may have strained, it must not break our bonds of affection. The mystic chords of memory, stretching from every battle-field, and patriot grave, to every living heart and hearthstone, all over this broad land, will yet swell the chorus of the Union, when again touched, as surely they will be, by the better angels of our nature."

As he spoke, Lincoln might have been wondering whether he had even a Cabinet to assist him in governing. William H. Seward, who had accepted Lincoln's tender of the post of Secretary of State, had asked two days before to be permitted to withdraw, and on Inauguration

Day Lincoln wrote him: "I am constrained to beg that you will countermand the withdrawal." Seward acceded to Lincoln's importunate request, but for weeks remained convinced that he, rather than the President, should run the government. As an ex-governor of New York and U.S. Senator for more than a decade, perhaps he may be forgiven for believing that he would dominate Lincoln and become the actual wielder of the power necessary to save the country. On April 1 he submitted a memorandum, "Some thoughts for the President's consideration," in which he proposed that "We are at the end of a month's administration and yet without a policy either domestic or foreign," and that he would be glad both to establish a policy and to prosecute it, if the President could not do so. Lincoln wrote out the following reply:

Executive Mansion April 1, 1861

Hon: W. H. Seward:

My dear Sir: Since parting with you I have been considering your paper dated this day, and entitled "Some thoughts for the President's consideration." The first proposition in it is, "1ste. We are at the end of a month's administration, and yet without a policy, either domestic or foreign."

At the *beginning* of that month, in the inaugural, I said "The power confided to me will be used to hold, occupy and possess the property and places belonging to the government, and to collect the duties, and imposts." This had your distinct approval at the time; and, taken in connection with the order I immediately gave General Scott, directing him to employ every means in his power to strengthen and hold the forts, comprises the exact domestic policy you now urge, with the single exception, that it does not propose to abandon Fort Sumter.

99

Inaugural portrait, February 23, 1861.

Again, I do not perceive how the re-inforcement of Fort Sumter would be done on a slavery, or party issue, while that of Fort Pickens would be on a more national, and patriotic one.

The news received yesterday in regard to St. Domingo, certainly brings a new item within the range of our foreign policy; but up to that time we have been preparing circulars, and instructions to ministers,

Mary Todd Lincoln in the gown she wore at the inaugural ball, March 4, 1861.

The inaugural procession (Frank Leslie's Illustrated Newspaper, *March 16, 1861*).

and the like, all in perfect harmony, without even a suggestion that we had no foreign policy.

Upon your closing propositions, that "whatever policy we adopt, there must be an energetic prosecution of it."

"For this purpose it must be somebody's business to pursue and direct it incessantly."

"Either the President must do it himself, and be all the while active in it, or"

"Devolve it on some member of his cabinet"

"Once adopted, debates on it must end, and all agree and abide" I remark that if this must be done, *I* must

do it. When a general line of policy is adopted, I apprehend there is no danger of its being changed without good reason, or continuing to be a subject of unnecessary debate; still, upon points arising in its progress, I wish, and suppose I am entitled to have the advice of all the cabinet. Your Obt. Servt.

A. Lincoln

Although Lincoln did not deliver this paper to Seward, he most certainly conveyed its substance. Thereafter Seward began to work in harness, and two months later wrote his wife, "Executive force and vigor are rare qualities. The President is the best of us."

Like Seward in believing he should have been President instead of Lincoln was Secretary of the Treasury Salmon P. Chase. Lincoln had appointed him to the post for similar as well as dissimilar reasons – on the one hand the man's demonstrated leadership of a strong segment of Abolitionist ex-Democrats, and on the other his religious, high-principled rectitude, which made him a strong if sanctimonious advocate of moral duty where Seward was suspect (to Chase at least) for his worldliness and his alliance with an allegedly corrupt New York political machine.

Although Lincoln's choice for Attorney General, Edward Bates of Missouri, had also been a hopeful candidate for the Republican nomination, he had no illusions about his responsibility to Lincoln. Born in Virginia while Washington was still President, and now an elder statesman of the old-line Whigs, he was perhaps closer to Lincoln than any other member of the Cabinet in political philosophy, believing slavery morally wrong and opposed to its extension, but agreed that the rights of slaveholders should be preserved in all the slave states. His selection for the Cabinet, Lincoln hoped, would aid in keeping the border slave states in the Union.

As a second anchor in the border states, Lincoln had chosen for Postmaster General, Montgomery Blair of Maryland, a Kentuckian by birth and the son of President Andrew Jackson's old crony, Francis Preston Blair. Like his Missouri brother Frank, who bore the father's name, Montgomery represented a family tradition of "the Union must be preserved," dating from Jackson's conflict with Senator John C. Calhoun of South Carolina, over "nullification," and both sons and father early fused with the Republicans in their respective states, where their antislavery sentiments made them subject to physical no less than political danger.

A Connecticut antislavery Democrat, Gideon Welles, represented Lincoln's New England choice for Secretary of the Navy. He was an able journalist and came to run the Navy Department with Yankee acumen and efficiency, if without other special qualifications. He kept a voluminous diary, a boon to later historians, in which Lincoln gradually emerges as the only figure in politics whose character Welles could respect without reservations.

Then, there was ex-Congressman Caleb Smith of Indiana, appointed Secretary of the Interior, a choice dictated by promises made by Lincoln's managers at the Chicago convention, in spite of Lincoln's instructions that no bargains were to be made. Ineffectual and in bad health, Smith was appointed to a federal judgeship after eighteen months of comparative failure at his post.

Finally, there was Senator Simon Cameron of Pennsylvania, whom Lincoln chose to be Secretary of War, also because he was committed by promises made by his managers at the Chicago convention. It had been said of Cameron by a fellow politician from Pennsylvania that "he would not steal a red hot stove." Cameron represented his state's industrial interests to the hilt and seemed to have no other commitments which could take precedence over them. Corruption discovered in war contracts forced his resignation and replacement by Edwin M. Stanton in January, 1862.

Stanton became one of Lincoln's most effective Cabinet members. An ardent Union Democrat, appointed Attorney General during the last months of Buchanan's administration, he had secretly informed Senator Seward of developments in Cabinet meetings, in order that the Unionists might not be caught off guard. Following Cameron's appointment by Lincoln, Stanton became

The cabinet: (top to bottom) Chase, Seward, Blair, Bates.

The cabinet: (top to bottom) Welles, Cameron, Stanton.

chief legal adviser to the Secretary of War. During the early months of the war, Stanton's undisguised contempt for Lincoln, whom he called "the original gorilla" and "the Illinois Ape," made him an incredible choice to many of Lincoln's supporters. Yet Lincoln saw in him the qualities of unquestionable loyalty to the cause, boundless energy, and complete integrity, which were so necessary to correct the corruption in awarding war contracts and to organize an efficient machinery for conducting the war. Although Stanton continued, in his relations with Lincoln, to be irascible and even disrespectful, Lincoln's good humor and firmness gradually won Stanton's grudging and finally wholehearted admiration.

Such was the group of men through and with whom Lincoln began to try to build a government on the shambles left by the Buchanan administration. Far more than in later years, when a hard core of Civil Service

remained to hold together the routine activities of the government during a shift in administrations, chaos reigned in every department, as duties devolved upon the greenest office seekers that patronage could bring forth. The pitifully small peacetime army was largely deprived of officers, many of whom were Southerners and had gone, or would shortly go, over to their respective states. Among these was Colonel Robert E. Lee, upon whom Lincoln had hoped to confer the general command, relieving the aged Virginian hero Winfield Scott, whose sole remaining value was as a symbol of fidelity to the Union.

The defecting officers had been abetted during the last days of the Buchanan administration by a Secretary of War who permitted and even arranged for military stores and weapons belonging to the United States to be taken over by the seceding states. Post offices and other

Federal property in these states had likewise been assumed by their governors. Only on the periphery of the new Confederacy were there a few remaining federal installations such as Fort Sumter, at the mouth of the harbor of Charleston, South Carolina, to which Lincoln could apply his avowed determination announced in his Inaugural Address, "to hold, occupy and possess the property and places belonging to the government." Among his Cabinet only Montgomery Blair categorically supported Lincoln's view that Sumter should be held if possible, and to that end provisioned, since the small besieged garrison was running out of food. Upon implementing this decision, Lincoln began the Civil War by sending provisions to Fort Sumter. On April 12, the batteries of South Carolina opened fire on the fort, and on April 14, the garrison surrendered. On April 15, Lincoln issued an order summoning 75,000 militia to put down the rebellion.

A great deal of historical ink has been spilled concerning Lincoln's moral responsibility for the Civil War. The ambiguity rests, in this instance as in that of Pearl Harbor, in the impossibility of establishing a neat dividing line between political and physical aggression, as well as between the aggressive act and the invitation to aggression which preceded it. Lincoln had always known that war is the extension of politics: to paraphrase his own expression, bullets instead of ballots. He had also put his view concerning the invitation to aggression into a metaphor in his speech at Cooper Union, "A highwayman holds a pistol to my ear, and mutters through his teeth, 'Stand and deliver or I shall kill you, and then you will be a murderer!'" In his position as President and within the principles so carefully delineated in his Inaugural Address, he could not do otherwise than try to hold Fort Sumter.

Lincoln's intention to save the Union required first of all that the border slave states be kept in it. Virginia was lost when, two days after Lincoln issued his call for troops, her state convention voted to secede. Governor John Letcher sent Virginia militia to seize the garrison at Harpers Ferry, and the small complement of Federal troops withdrew, as did the naval forces at Norfolk. Delaware, the most northern slave state, made no move to secede, nor did Maryland. In the latter, however, secession sympathy was so strong that mobs formed in Baltimore to attack the Sixth Massachusetts Infantry on its way to defend the nation's capital, and a number were killed. Various delegations of prominent Maryland citizens urged that no more troops be brought through their state. "I must have troops," Lincoln replied, ". . . our men are not moles. . . . They are not birds. . . . There is no way but to march across, and that they must do."

111

"Wanting to work is so rare a want, ..."

But he delayed further troop movements until the state, predominantly Union in sentiment, had re-established civil control.

Kentucky and Missouri were the most divided states. Families split on the question of where loyalty lay. Mary Todd Lincoln's own family was typical, with one brother and a half-sister loyal Unionists, one brother and three half-brothers going over to the Confederacy, and three half-sisters married to men who becaume Confederate officers. It was Lincoln's fear that "to lose Kentucky is nearly ... to lose the whole game." In reply to Lincoln's call for troops, Governor Beriah Magoffin telegraphed, "Kentucky will furnish no troops for the wicked purpose of subduing her sister Southern states." Whereupon Lincoln sent the loyal Kentuckian who had commanded Fort Sumter, Robert Anderson, now promoted

President Lincoln and General Winfield Scott reviewing a regiment. Sketch by Alfred Waud.

to Brigadier General, to take charge of recruiting at Cincinnati, just across the Ohio, and made arrangements through his old friend Joshua Speed and other loyal Kentuckians to distribute arms in support of their cause. This paid off in June when Kentucky elected nine Union Congressmen against one secessionist.

In Missouri, Governor Claiborne Jackson and a secessionist legislature were admitted to the Confederacy, but loyal Unionists led by Frank Blair and Captain Nathaniel Lyon managed to keep control of the state, where some of the bloodiest early battles were fought, and where "bushwhacking" guerrilla forces on both sides continued throughout the war to prey upon former friends and neighbors. Even in the early years of the twentieth century there still remained symbols of this internecine slaughter – the chimneys of a loyal Union farmhouse

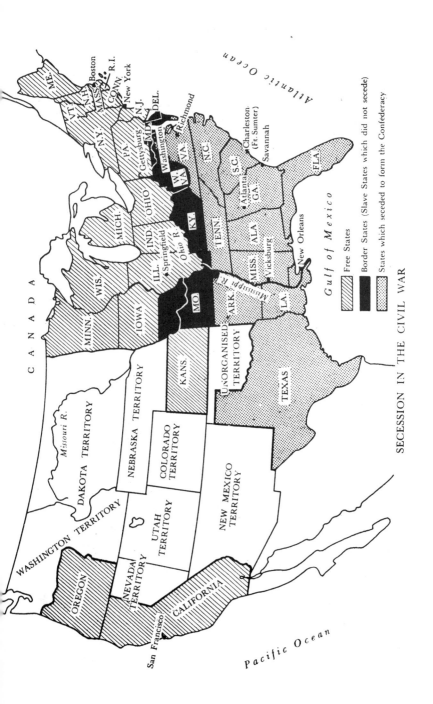

CANADA

Atlantic Ocean

ME.

N.H.
VT.
MASS. Boston
CONN. R.I.
New York
N.J.
DEL.

N.Y.

PA.
Gettysburg
Washington
MD.
Richmond
VA.
W. VA.

N.C.

Charleston
(Ft. Sumter)
S.C.
Savannah

OHIO

IND.

ILL.
Springfield
Ohio R.

KY.

TENN.

ALA.

GA.

FLA.

MICH.

WIS.

MINN.

IOWA

MO.

KANS.

UNORGANISED
TERRITORY

ARK.

MISS.
Vicksburg

LA.

New Orleans

Mississippi R.

Atlanta

Gulf of Mexico

DAKOTA TERRITORY

NEBRASKA TERRITORY

COLORADO
TERRITORY

NEW MEXICO
TERRITORY

TEXAS

Missouri R.

WASHINGTON TERRITORY

UTAH
TERRITORY

OREGON

NEVADA
TERRITORY

CALIFORNIA

San Francisco

Pacific Ocean

SECESSION IN THE CIVIL WAR

Free States

Border States (Slave States which did not secede)

States which seceded to form the Confederacy

in a secessionist community, kept painted red, white, and blue in defiance, after half a century. It was in Missouri and Kentucky that Lincoln began to win a war that would require four more years of hard fighting.

4

In the beginning the Confederacy was better prepared. The seceding states early began to collect war materials (largely from Federal garrisons) and to enlist troops. The cream of West Point trained officers – Robert E. Lee, "Stonewall" Jackson, J. E. B. Stuart, Albert Sidney Johnston, Joseph E. Johnston, and James Longstreet, to name only a few – went with their states. They were career officers who, for reasons of tradition and social milieu, were more numerous among Southern than among Northern graduates of the Military Academy. Their Northern counterparts, men like George B. McClellan, Ulysses S. Grant, and William T. Sherman, for example, had gone into industry or business after serving a few years in army posts. Lincoln had first to "find" his generals, and then try them out, hit or miss, until he knew which ones could perform.

As the conflict developed during the next four years, the story for long seemed a sad one. Lincoln gradually succeeded in building the greatest army the world had ever known, in organizing the industrial and commercial complex of the North to supply the war effort and at the same time do business as usual both at home and abroad, in maintaining a fairly stable, if booming, economy, and in keeping political control in his own hands in spite of ambitious finagling by members of his own Cabinet like Chase and by political generals like John C. Frémont and George B. McClellan.

The South, however, won most of the early battles. In the East the war remained a continual stalemate, to

Robert E. Lee.

some extent because of incompetent Union commanders, but also because of the terrain east of the Allegheny Mountains. A look at the map of Virginia will show the rivers and estuaries which stacked the odds in favor of defense, whether by Lee or by McClellan, and helped make it a war of engineers. In the West, the rivers provided avenues for invasion, and it was along these that Grant and Sherman began to penetrate the Confederacy in a series of campaigns which spelled ultimate success.

Greatly contributing to the eventual success of the Union armies was the Union navy's successful blockade of Southern ports. Simultaneous with his call for troops, Lincoln had issued an order blockading all ports in the seceding states. Unlike the army, the navy was officered principally by Northern men, and whereas the seceding states took over the harbors on their coast, the ships that had used them remained with the Union. To these, Secretary of the Navy Gideon Welles added as rapidly as possible, purchasing, converting, and building warships to maintain the blockade which would prevent the Confederacy from importing war supplies or exporting the cotton necessary to pay for them. In addition the merchant fleet was expanded, and gunboats were built to operate on the western rivers in support of the troops advancing southward. To this effort the Confederacy made a romantic but generally futile response with a few privateers and blockade runners, and wrought minor havoc with the pioneering ironclad *Merrimac* in the waters around Norfolk, until the Union ironclad *Monitor*

Stonewall Jackson.

put a stop to that in March, 1862. If the outcome of the war on land was ever in doubt, the outcome at sea was settled from the start.

5

From the beginning it was apparent that the prime cause of the war, slavery, must be abolished. The questions were "how?" and "when?" The answers to these questions Lincoln constantly sought, but only as they could be arrived at subordinate to the answer to the more important question of how to save the Union. In his Message to Congress in Special Session, July 4, 1861, Lincoln had defined the war as "essentially a people's contest."

Our popular government has often been called an experiment. Two points in it our people have already settled – the successful *establishing* and the successful

William T. Sherman.

Ulysses S. Grant.

administering of it. One still remains – its successful *maintenance* against a formidable internal attempt to overthrow it. It is now for them to demonstrate to the world that those who can fairly carry an election can also suppress a rebellion; that ballots are the rightful and peaceful successors of bullets; and that when ballots have fairly and constitutionally decided, there can be no successful appeal back to bullets; that there can be no successful appeal except to ballots themselves, at succeeding elections. . . . No compromise by public servants could in this case be a cure; not that compromises are not often proper, but that no popular government can long survive a marked precedent that those who carry an election can only save the Government from immediate destruction by giving up the

119

main point upon which the people gave the election. The people themselves, and not their servants, can safely reverse their own deliberate decisions.

Thus, when in September, 1861 General Frémont in command of the Department of the West in Missouri issued a proclamation freeing the slaves in the area under his command, Lincoln countermanded the proclamation, and in answer to his old friend Senator Orville H. Browning of Illinois, who protested that Frémont's action was the only means of saving the government, Lincoln maintained: "On the contrary it is itself the surrender of the government. Can it be pretended that it is any longer the Government of the U.S. – any government of Constitution and laws, – wherein a General, or a President, may make permanent rules of property by proclamation?"

On the other hand, the act passed by Congress confiscating "property used for insurrectionary purposes," approved August 6, 1861, had in fact freed many escaped slaves of Confederate owners by confiscating them, and the slaves thus freed became known as "contrabands." It was Lincoln's hope that the loyal slave states might be persuaded to pass legislation freeing the slaves owned by their respective citizens and compensating the owners. To this end he sent a Message to Congress on March 6, 1862, recommending adoption of a Joint Resolution promising co-operation and pecuniary aid to the states which might adopt "gradual abolishment of slavery." The resolution was adopted on April 10.

On May 9 General David Hunter, in command of the Department of the South with headquarters at Hilton Head, South Carolina, issued an order of Military Emancipation, similar to the earlier one issued by Frémont but different in that it applied to no loyal state, freeing the slaves in Georgia, Florida, and South Carolina.

121

President Lincoln with Allàn Pinkerton and General John A. McClernand at Antietam, October, 1862.

This also Lincoln revoked in a Proclamation dated May 19, declaring that "whether it be competent for me, as Commander-in-Chief of the Army and Navy, to declare the Slaves of any state, or states, free, and whether at any time, in any case, it shall have become a necessity indispensable to the maintenance of the government, to exercise such posed power, are questions which, under my responsibility, I reserve to myself . . . ."

Great disappointment reigned among antislavery forces throughout the North. Delegations memorialized, committees called on Lincoln, and influential individuals wrote him, all with a single theme – abolish slavery. On July 12, following the adjournment of Congress, Lincoln invited the Representatives and Senators of the border states to the Executive Mansion and ap-

Union private.

Confederate private.

pealed to them to work for "a *decision* at once to emancipate *gradually*." The Representatives and Senators of the border states not only objected to the expense of compensated emancipation but argued that emancipation in any form would increase the spirit of rebellion. Caught thus between two forces, Lincoln decided to issue (July 25) a proclamation warning all persons in rebellion to cease and "return to their proper allegiance . . . on pain of the forfeitures and seizures" of their property, including slaves. This infuriated all those who were crying for action, but particularly Horace Greeley, who published a bitter open letter in the New York *Tribune* of August 20, entitled "The Prayer of Twenty Millions." Lincoln replied on August 22:

Executive Mansion,
Washington, August 22, 1862.

Hon. Horace Greeley:
Dear Sir

I have just read yours of the 19th addressed to myself through the New-York Tribune. If there be in it any statements, or assumptions of fact, which I may know to be erroneous, I do not, now and here, controvert them. If there be in it any inferences which I may believe to be falsely drawn, I do not now and here, argue against them. If there be perceptible in it an impatient and dictatorial tone, I waive it in deference to an old friend, whose heart I have always supposed to be right.

As to the policy I "seem to be pursuing" as you say, I have not meant to leave any one in doubt.

I would save the Union. I would save it the shortest

Confederate dead at Antietam.

way under the Constitution. The sooner the national authority can be restored; the nearer the Union will be "the Union as it was." If there be those who would not save the Union, unless they could at the same time *save* slavery, I do not agree with them. If there be those who would not save the Union unless they could at the same time *destroy* slavery, I do not agree with them. My paramount object in this struggle is to save the Union, and is *not* either to save or to destroy slavery. If I could save the Union without freeing *any* slave I would do it, and if I could save it by freeing all the slaves I would do it; and if I could save it by freeing some and leaving others alone I would also do that. What I do about slavery, and the colored race, I do because I believe it helps to save the Union; and what I forbear, I forbear because I do *not* believe it would help to save the Union. I shall do *less* when-

ever I shall believe what I am doing hurts the cause, and I shall do *more* whenever I shall believe doing more will help the cause. I shall try to correct errors when shown to be errors; and I shall adopt new views so fast as they shall appear to be true views.

I have here stated my purpose according to my view of *official* duty; and I intend no modification of my oft-expressed *personal* wish that all men every where could be free. Yours,

A. Lincoln

If Lincoln's sense of frustration in his efforts to hew to the line of his conservative policy in regard to slavery was not enough, his despondency at repeated failures in military operations, climaxed during the last days of August by defeat at the Second Battle of Bull Run, added the necessary shove that pushed him to the point of accepting his last resort. His frame of mind at this point is indicated by a note written by Attorney General Edward Bates on September 2: "The Prest. was in deep distress . . . he seemed wrung by the bitterest anguish – said he felt almost ready to hang himself. . ." Even more revealing is the following fragment, probably written by Lincoln on the same day:

The will of God prevails. In great contests each party claims to act in accordance with the will of God. Both *may* be, and one *must* be wrong. God can not be *for,* and *against* the same thing at the same time. In the present civil war it is quite possible that God's purpose is something different from the purpose of either party – and yet the human instrumentalities, working just as they do, are of the best adaptation to effect His purpose. I am almost ready to say this is probably true – that God wills this contest, and wills that it shall not end yet. By his mere quiet power, on the minds of the now contestants, He could have either *saved* or *destroyed* the Union without a human contest. Yet the contest began. And having begun He could give the final victory to either side any day. Yet the contest proceeds.

On September 22, Lincoln called the Cabinet together to announce his decision to issue the Preliminary Emancipation Proclamation which would declare his purpose to proclaim on January 1, 1863, that "... all persons held as slaves within any state, or designated part of a state, the people whereof shall then be in rebellion ... shall be then, thenceforward, and forever free. ..." He did not wish the advice of the Cabinet on the question of desi-

Powder monkey on U. S. S. "New Hampshire."

rability – his mind was made up – but he would entertain suggestions on the wording of the draft he had prepared. At long last, as a necessity of war, he took the symbolic step as Chief Executive which he had always hoped and believed the people would ultimately take through the means provided in the Constitution, and which he still recognized could not be of permanent effect unless and until ratified by the people, according to due constitutional process, toward which he would continue to direct his efforts. He concluded his Annual Message to Congress on December 1 with a further plea for adoption of articles amending the Constitution to provide for conpensated emancipation:

Cartoon (Punch, *October, 1862*).

ABE LINCOLN'S LAST CARD; OR, ROUGE-ET-NOIR.

By the President of the United States of America

A Proclamation.

Whereas, on the twenty-second day of September, in the year of our Lord one thousand eight hundred and sixty-two, a proclamation was issued by the President of the United States, containing, among other things, the following, to wit:

"That on the first day of January, in the year of our Lord one thousand eight hundred and sixty-three, all persons held as slaves within any State or designated part of a State, the people whereof shall then be in rebellion against the United States, shall be then, thenceforward, and forever free; and the Executive Government of the United States, including the military and naval authority thereof, will recognize and maintain the freedom of such persons, and will do no act or acts to repress such persons, or any of them, in any efforts they may make for their actual freedom.

"That the Executive will, on the first day

The Emancipation Proclamation (first page).

Fellow-citizens, *we* cannot escape history. We of this Congress and this administration, will be remembered in spite of ourselves. No personal significance, or insignificance, can spare one or another of us. The fiery trial through which we pass, will light us down, in honor or dishonor, to the latest generation. We *say* we are for the Union. The world will not forget that we say this. We know how to save the Union. The world knows we do know how to save it. We – even *we here* – hold the power, and bear the responsibility. In *giving* freedom to the *slave,* we assure freedom to the *free* – honorable alike in what we give, and what we preserve. We shall nobly save, or meanly lose, the last best, hope of earth. Other means may succeed; this could not fail. The way is plain, peaceful, generous, just – a way which, if followed, the world will forever applaud, and God must forever bless.

6

Had not the crushing military, political, and administrative decisions so constantly kept his mind and nerves at the highest pitch of preoccupation, Lincoln's family problems and personal tragedy might have driven him to despair of their own weight. Mary Lincoln had never been "accepted," on the one hand, by the Southern-sympathizing society of the nation's capital, who regarded her, a Kentuckian from a slaveholding family, as a traitor to their cause. On the other hand, the wives of the new antislavery Republican circle gossiped about her "secesh" relatives and even whispered that she was disloyal herself. This went so far as to start rumors of her spying for the Confederacy, which became the subject of investigation by a Congressional commitee. The President found it necessary to assure the committee personally that he knew his wife was loyal.

Ambitious Mary also engaged in politics and was used by conniving persons like Governor William Sprague of Rhode Island and James Gordon Bennett, editor of the New York *Herald*, in an effort to influence Lincoln's choices for important posts. Her quick temper and sharp tongue assisted her in making enemies even in Lincoln's official family – notably with Lincoln's secretaries John G. Nicolay and John Hay, who privately called her "hell cat," and with Secretary of War Edwin M. Stanton, and Secretary of State William H. Seward, whom she once called "a dirty abolitionist sneak."

Then there were her troubles in trying to make the Executive Mansion run on pitifully inadequate allow-

With his secretaries John G. Nicolay and John Hay.

ances. She became involved in debts which she tried to cover up. In the opinion of her son Robert in later years, money was one subject on which his mother was "not mentally responsible."

Mary, like her husband when he had time, was a fond and indulgent parent and a friend to her son's friends. Though Robert, at Harvard, was no particular problem, the two younger boys, William age eleven and Thomas (Tad) age eight when they arrived in the White House, were typical boys, full of pranks and fond of their prerogative of making the Executive Mansion "home," playing on the roof and in the attic, littering the lawn with pets – ponies, goats, cats, dogs, and even rabbits. Both parents believed the boys should "have a good time." Children of the era, they played at war, sentencing a favorite doll, dressed as a Zouave, to death for sleeping on picket duty, and obtaining an official pardon on

With his son Thomas (Tad), February, 1864.

White House portraits, 1862 and 1863.

Executive Mansion stationery: "The doll Jack is pardoned. By order of the President. A. Lincoln." In this Secretary Stanton became involved, commissioning Tad a lieutenant and giving him a full uniform, which Tad took seriously enough on one occasion to assert his authority by dismissing the White House guards.

When Mary and the boys were away from home, Lincoln was lonely. One letter, written in August, 1863, while Lincoln was escaping the heat by staying at the Soldiers' Home in the environs of Washington, tells of domestic matters, including a sad item for Tad. "Tell dear Tad, poor 'Nanny Goat' is lost; and Mrs. Cuthbert [the housekeeper] & I are in distress about it. The day you left Nanny was found resting herself, and chewing her little cud, on the middle of Tad's bed. But now she's gone! The gardener kept complaining that she destroyed the flowers, till it was concluded to bring her down to the White House. This was done, and the second day

133

she had disappeared, and has not been heard of since. This is the last we know of poor 'Nanny.'"

When Willie died of a fever in February, 1862, his mother became temporarily deranged with grief. One of the saddest episodes of the weeks that followed tells of the President, arm about his wife's waist, pointing through the window to the insane asylum in the distance with the words, "Mother, try and control your grief, or it will drive you mad, and we may have to send you there." Of the President's own sorrow, there are records also, none more telling than an episode recounted by a military visitor who found Lincoln reading Shakespeare's *King John*. The President read aloud the lines in Act III where Constance laments her lost son:

And, father cardinal, I have heard you say
That we shall see and know our friends in heaven.
If that be true, I shall see my boy again. . . .

"Colonel, did you ever dream of a lost friend and feel you were holding sweet communion with that friend, and yet have a sad consciousness that it was not a reality? – just so I dream of my boy Willie."

But life went on, and Lincoln sought relief, when he could, in reading his favorite Shakespearean plays, or in attending the theater, of which he had become very fond. He was aware that his critics made the most of this as a supposed example of the President's indifference to the nation's sorrows. On one occasion he took note of his critics with the remark, "I must have a change of some sort or die." He was also fond of reading the popular humorists of the day, and on one occasion insisted on reading at a Cabinet meeting Artemus Ward's "High-Handed Outrage at Utica." When no one laughed, Lincoln became solemn, "Why don't you laugh?" he asked.

Executive Mansion,
Washington, Nov. 11, 1865.

Hon. Secretary of War
My dear Sir:
I personally wish
Jacob R. Freese, of New Jersey
to be appointed a Colonel for
a colored regiment — and
this regardless of whether he can
tell the exact shade of Julius
Caesar's hair.
Yours truly
A. Lincoln

"With the fearful strain that is on me night and day, if I did not laugh occasionally I should die, and you need this medicine as much as I."

He continued to crack jokes and tell the stories and anecdotes which had made him famous among raconteurs in Illinois long before he became a figure on the national scene. Sometimes it was a means of sidetracking importunate visitors, such as the general who requested the release from prison of an old friend. Lincoln was reminded of a group of boys and girls who went "Maying" and having crossed a creek in a boat found the boat gone upon their return. Each boy picked up his favorite girl and carried her across, leaving one odd couple, a short squat boy and a great "Gothic built" old maid. "You are trying to leave me in the same predicament," Lincoln said. "You fellows are all getting your friends out of this scrape . . . until nobody but Jeff Davis

135

and myself will be left. . . . How should I look, lugging him over?" Sometimes he used a story to kill a specious argument, such as the sentimental plea that if slaves were freed both slaves and masters would starve because slaves could not work without overseers and masters deprived of slaves would be unable to make a living. This reminded Lincoln of an old farmer who planted potatoes and turned his hogs into the patch to root them out. When a neighbor asked what the hogs would do when the ground froze, the farmer replied, "Well, it may come pretty hard on their snouts, but I guess it will be 'root, hog, or die!'" Sometimes his humor was in a flashing twist of his informant's intentions, as when he replied to a temperance criticism of General Grant's fondness for whisky, that he would like to know General Grant's brand to recommend to some of his other generals; or when, asked for a suitable motto to engrave on the new greenback currency, he suggested ironically, "Silver and gold have I none, but such as I have I give thee." If Lincoln's humor did not save the Union, it certainly saved his own sanity and helped him straighten out many a loyal Unionist who "couldn't see the woods for the trees."

7

Fighting a war to preserve the Union might have been simpler if the North had been united, or if the Republican Party which had nominated and elected Lincoln had been, or if, at the barest minimum, the administration itself had been. There was, however, little unanimity on any subject except the very general notion that the Union should be preserved. A large portion of the Democratic Party were open in their opposition to all measures which Lincoln undertook, and many were out-and-out secession sympathizers, who came to be designated "Copperheads" with something less than respect to the snake which suggested their name. On the one hand, the Copperheads constantly played up the horrors of the war, lamented the ghastly losses in dead and wounded, and on the other, held out open arms to guerrilla invasions and spies. Most conspicuous among their leaders was Representative Clement L. Vallandigham of Ohio, who was judiciously exiled to the Confederacy by Lincoln following his arrest and conviction of treason in May, 1863. A man of mettle, Vallandigham ran the blockade, escaped to Canada, and campaigned for the governorship of Ohio from across the border, with the help of not a few newspapers interested in preserving freedom of the press and in denouncing Lincoln's "dictatorial" suspension of the writ of habeas corpus, an act which Lincoln defended by asking, "Must I shoot a simple-minded soldier boy who deserts, while I touch not a hair of a wiley agitator who induces him to desert?" Nevertheless, when Vallandigham crossed the border and began stumping the country, inciting mobs and vicious riots and preaching the secession of the Western and Northwestern states. he was permitted to continue, and became in August, 1864, the leading figure on the stage of the Democratic National Convention which nominated General George B. McClellan as its candidate for the presidency, on a peace platform in which one of the planks characterized the war as a failure and demanded that "immediate efforts be made for a cessation of hostilities."

In the Republican Party the factions frequently seemed more interested in destroying each other than in destroying the enemy. Generally there were the Conservatives – Lincoln men who supported the war effort and Lincoln's mild reconstruction policies in the conquered areas, but dragged their feet on emancipation; and the

Radicals – Abolitionists and Jacobins who advocated the ruthless destruction of the ruling class in the South. In the Senate and House of Representatives the Radicals became so strong in their resolve to force the resignation of Secretary Seward, who represented the Conservative element, that Lincoln was able to preserve his own faithful Secretary of State only by maneuvering Secretary of the Treasury Chase, the darling of the Radicals, into offering his resignation. With both letters of resignation in hand, Lincoln said, "Now I can ride; I have got a pumpkin in each end of my bag." Neither resignation was accepted.

As the election year 1864 began, it was an open question whether Lincoln could be nominated again, and if nominated, elected. The name of the Republican Party had fallen into such popular disrepute that the Conservatives, particularly the Blair element, sought a new name under which to call a convention – the National Union Party. Although the ascendancy of the Radicals was in part responsible for the unpopularity of Republicanism, the more fundamental causes were the series of military reverses, or rather failures to achieve victories while sustaining terrific losses in dead and wounded. The Wilderness campaign which began early in May, 1864, following Lincoln's appointment of Grant as commander of all the Union armies, proved to be the bloodiest of the war, and Grant became known as "the butcher," especially after the climax early in June at Cold Harbor, where the Union forces lost 7,000 killed in a single hour of fighting.

Although there was a rump movement to nominate and elect General John C. Frémont, which collapsed when Frémont withdrew his candidacy, the most serious effort to displace Lincoln was led by Secretary of the Treasury Chase. Unlike Seward and Stanton, both of

whom became convinced of Lincoln's ability and gave him loyal personal as well as official support, Chase remained from the beginning determined to become Lincoln's successor. He was convinced, in his utterly pious self-esteem, that he alone in the entire administration possessed the intellectual and moral capabilities necessary to the job. His Diary and his letters reveal the most complete self-delusion that genuine ability can lead a man into when blinded by egotism. They reveal over and over his condescension toward Lincoln as an inferior: slow of mentality, indecisive, but kindly in a crude way, whose occasional success was derived from the advice of his Secretary of the Treasury, the brains of the entire administration. Chase wrote, "the administration cannot be continued as it is, for properly speaking there is in fact no administration. There are departments and there is a President. The latter leaves administration substantially to the heads of the former, deciding himself comparatively few questions." And concerning his own department he admitted in February, 1864, "I think I have made few mistakes. Indeed . . . I am not able to see where, if I had to do my work all over again, I could in any manner do otherwise than I have."

Chase maintained an overt stance of propriety, saying and writing the things which could not be taken as insubordination but which would nevertheless encourage others to attack the President at all the weakest points of his administration, purported or real; and he kept up a constant and discreet undercover direction of the Radical attacks on the President. Gideon Welles described Chase's maneuvers aptly by contrasting his activities with those of the Blairs: "Warfare with them is open, bold and unsparing. With Chase it is silent, persistent, but regulated with discretion. Blairs make no false pretensions. Chase avows no enmities." Fully aware of Chase's ambition as well as his activities, Lincoln never-

Private   Executive Mansion,
                                Washington, March 13, 1864.
Hon. Michael Hahn
     My dear Sir:
              I congratulate you on having fixed
your name in history as the first free-state Governor
of Louisiana. Now you are about to have a Convention which, among other things, will probably define
the elective franchise. I barely suggest for your private consideration, whether some of the colored people may not be let in— as, for instance, the very in-
telligent, and especially those who have fought gal-
lantly in our ranks. They would probably help, in some
trying-time to come, to keep the jewel of liberty within
the family of freedom. But this is only a suggestion,
not to the public, but to you alone.
                              Yours truly
                                  A. Lincoln

theless respected the over-all energy, efficiency, and honesty with which the Treasury Department was run. When the subject of Chase's presidential ambition was raised, Lincoln likened the Secretary of the Treasury to a plough horse bitten by a "chin fly" – there was no point in knocking off the fly when that was just what was needed to make the horse pull!

The time came, however, when Chase's pretensions and the activities of his supporters became too mutually embarrassing for either Chase or Lincoln to ignore them further. A particularly vicious circular appeared, bearing the name of Radical Senator Samuel C. Pomeroy of Kansas, but purportedly written by Chase himself, attacking Lincoln and avocating Chase for "the qualities needed in a Presidential candidate." On February 22, 1864, Chase wrote Lincoln a letter categorically denying that he had any knowledge of the circular before he saw it in print and expressing regret and fear that "such use of my name might impair my usefulness as Head of the Treasury Department." Lincoln replied a week later, "I fully concur with you that neither of us can be justly held responsible for what our respective friends may do without our instigation or countenance. . . . Whether you shall remain at the head of the Treasury Department is a question which I will not allow myself to consider from any stand-point other than my judgment of the public service; and, in that view, I do not perceive occasion for a change." The popular reaction to the circular was so intense, however, that Chase's hopes were virtually destroyed, and in March he publicly withdrew his name, but only, as he emphasized, through a sense of duty to the cause, and in spite of the urgent demands of his friends. His unctuous manner of withdrawal brought forth the quip from Senator Edwin D. Morgan of New York: "Mr. Chase will subside as a candidate after the nomina-

RUNNING

E "MACHINE".

tion is made, not before."

The Republican National Union Convention renominated Lincoln in June without serious opposition, in spite of great anti-Lincoln sentiment among the Radical delegates, simply because there was no other candidate who could command a remote possibility of success. There were too many staunch Lincoln supporters in every state in the North, particularly among the common citizens who agreed with Lincoln that preserving the Union was the all-encompassing purpose of the war. On June 29, Chase again handed Lincoln his resignation and this time Lincoln accepted it, again commending Chase's "ability and fidelity," but concluding, ". . . you and I have reached a point of mutual embarrassment in our official relation which it seems can not be overcome, or longer sustained, consistently with the public service."

From June until August, the fortunes of war showed no marked improvement, and late in August Lincoln himself began to doubt that he could carry the campaign against the heavy swell of the Democratic "peace" movement to nominate and elect General McClellan, and negotiate the cessation of the war and the recognition of the Confederacy. On August 23, Lincoln wrote the following memorandum and sealed it up: "This morning, as for some days past, it seems exceedingly probable that this Administration will not be re-elected. Then it will be my duty to so co-operate with the President-elect, as to save the Union between the election and the inauguration; as he will have secured his election on such ground that he can not possibly save it afterwards." At the Cabinet meeting held on the same day, he asked each of his Cabinet members to sign the back of the sealed sheet.

At the Cabinet meeting held on November 11, following his re-election three days before, Lincoln opened the memorandum, read it, and commented, "I resolved,

in the case of the election of General McClellan ...
that I would see him and talk matters over with him.
I would say, 'General, the election has demonstrated
that you are stronger, have more influence with the
American people than I. Now let us together, you with
your influence and I with all the executive power of
the Government, try to save the country. You raise as
many troops as you possibly can for this final trial, and
I will devote all my energies to assisting and finishing
the war.'"

To this Secretary Seward replied, "And the General
would answer you, 'Yes, Yes'; and the next day when
you saw him again and pressed these views upon him,
he would say, 'Yes, Yes'; and so on forever, and would
have done nothing at all."

Executive Mansion
Washington, Aug. 23, 1864.

*This morning, as for some days past,
it seems exceedingly probable that
this Administration will not be re-
elected. Then it will be my duty
to so co-operate with the President
elect, as to save the Union between
the election and the inauguration;
as he will have secured his election on such ground that he cannot
possibly save it afterwards.*

A. Lincoln

145

Lincoln considers the probability of defeat in the election of 1864.

"At least," Lincoln replied, "I should have done my duty and have stood clear before my own conscience. . . ."

In the election, Lincoln's loyal supporters had given him 55.09 per cent of the total votes cast and had carried all the states, including the newly admitted state of Nevada, with the exception of Kentucky, Delaware, and New Jersey. But perhaps the most heartening thing of all to Lincoln was the fact that the soldier vote was overwhelmingly in his favor.

What had happened between August and November to reverse so pessimistic an outlook as Lincoln's memorandum of August 23? The answer is: a resounding military success in the Shenandoah Valley, laid waste by the army commanded by General Philip Sheridan. The climax came with the General's famous wild ride that turned an apparent defeat on October 20 at Cedar Creek into one of the most spectacular victories of the war.

When Lincoln responded from the White House balcony to an election victory serenade on the night of November 10, he may well have wondered what the verdict might have been had Federal law specified the first Tuesday following the first Monday in September, rather than November, as the day on which presidential elections are held.

It has long been a grave question whether any government, not *too* strong for the liberties of its people, can be strong *enough* to maintain its own existence, in great emergencies.

On this point the present rebellion brought our republic to a severe test; and a presidential election occurring in regular course during the rebellion added not a little to the strain. If the loyal people, *united,* were put to the utmost of their strength by the rebellion, must they not fail when *divided,* and partially

paralyzed, by a war among themselves?

But the election was a necessity.

We can not have free government without elections; and if the rebellion could force us to forego, or postpone a national election, it might fairly claim to have already conquered and ruined us. The strife of the election is but human nature practically applied to the facts of the case. What has occurred in this case, must ever recur in similar cases. Human nature will not change. In any future great national trial, compared with the men of this, we shall have as weak, and as strong; as silly and as wise; as bad and good. Let us, therefore, study the incidents of this, as philosophy to learn wisdom from, and none of them as wrongs to be revenged.

But the election, along with its incidental, and undesirable strife, has done good too. It has demonstrated that a people's government can sustain a na-

147

Cartoon (Harper's Weekly, *November 26, 1864*).

tional election, in the midst of a great civil war. Until now it has not been known to the world thas this was a possibility. It shows also how *sound,* and how *strong* we still are. It shows that, even among candidates of the same party, he who is most devoted to the Union, and most opposed to treason, can receive most of the people's votes. It shows also, to the extent yet known, that we have more men now, than we had when the war began. Gold is good in its place; but living, brave, patriotic men, are better than gold.

But the rebellion continues; and now that the election is over, may not all, having a common interest, re-unite in a common effort, to save our common country? For my own part I have striven, and shall strive to avoid placing any obstacle in the way. So long as I have been here I have not willingly planted a thorn in any man's bosom.

While I am deeply sensible to the high compliment of a re-election; and duly grateful, as I trust, to Almighty God for having directed my countrymen to a right conclusion, as I think, for their own good, it adds nothing to my satisfaction that any other man be disappointed or pained by the result.

May I ask those who have not differed with me, to join with me, in this same spirit towards those who have?

And now, let me close by asking three hearty cheers for our brave soldiers and seamen and their gallant and skilful commanders.

8

Considering the crowded day-by-day calendar of Lincoln's official duties, the literary distinction of his speeches, messages to Congress, and letters, is, to put it bluntly, the most incredible fact of his Presidency. Even

Union dead at Gettysburg.

when we recognized the long development and the care for matching of words with thought and feeling which established Lincoln's early skill, the fact remains that he continued under great difficulties to maintain and even surpass his own high standard of literary accomplishment. He meant to govern but also to leave a record in his own words, some of which might last longer perhaps than the nation itself. He not only wrote out his speeches and messages to Congress, in the latter incorporating, revising, and adapting, of course, portions supplied in draft by members of his Cabinet; but also the letters which have become famous, sometimes working far into the night to get them done. Although the bulk of routine correspondence could be answered and signed by his secretaries in their own names "for the President," or turned over to the proper Cabinet member for attention, frequently with a felicitous endorsement in Lincoln's own hand, in no instance was there a major speech or communication which he was willing to delegate to be ghost-written by any of his aides.

Some of his best letters were strictly personal, while others were public, in the sense that he expected others than the immediate recipient to read them. Two letters of condolence illustrate the care with which he composed both kinds. The first was written to Fanny McCullough, daughter of his old friend Colonel William McCullough of Bloomington, Illinois, who had organized the 4th Illinois Cavalry. The second was written to Mrs. Lydia Bixby of Boston, Massachusetts, a widow about whom he knew only the supposed facts, furnished him by the War Department with the suggestion that he write her a letter which would in a manner recognize the ultimate personal sacrifice of so many mothers.

> Executive Mansion,
> Washington, December 23, 1862.

Dear Fanny

It is with deep grief that I learn of the death of your kind and brave Father; and, especially, that it is affecting your young heart beyond what is common in such cases. In this sad world of ours, sorrow comes to all; and, to the young, it comes with bitterest agony, because it takes them unawares. The older have learned to ever expect it. I am anxious to afford some alleviation to your present distress. Perfect relief is not possible, except with time. You can not now realize that you will ever feel better. Is not this so? And yet it is a mistake. You are sure to be happy again. To know this, which is certainly true, will make you some less miserable now. I have had experience enough to know what I say; and you need only to believe it, to feel better at once. The memory of your dear Father, instead of an agony, will yet be a sad sweet feeling in your heart, of a purer, and holier sort than you have known before.

Please present my kind regards to your afflicted mother.

Your sincere friend A. Lincoln.

Miss. Fanny McCullough.

Executive Mansion,
Washington, Nov. 21, 1864.

Dear Madam, – I have been shown in the files of the War Department a statement of the Adjutant General of Massachusetts, that you are the mother of five sons who have died gloriously on the field of battle.

I feel how weak and fruitless must be any words of mine which should attempt to beguile you from the grief of a loss so overwhelming. But I cannot refrain

Joseph Hooker.

from tendering you the consolation that may be found in the thanks of the Republic they died to save.

I pray that our Heavenly Father may assuage the anguish of your bereavement, and leave you only the cherished memory of the loved and lost, and the solemn pride that must be yours, to have laid so costly a sacrifice upon the altar of Freedom. Yours, very sincerely and respectfully,

A. Lincoln.

Mrs. Bixby.

Some of his letters and telegrams to his generals remain the unique gold nuggets of history washed down by the war with the sands of innumerable official documents which historians have sifted and will continue to sift in future generations. There is little that the historian can do but mount them in a proper setting, as old prospectors were wont to mount their unique find on a ring or stickpin to remind them of just how it was. Such are the two following letters. The first was written to General Joseph Hooker, who replaced General Ambrose E. Burnside, who had replaced General George B. McClellan, who had replaced General John Pope, who had first replaced General McClellan, in Lincoln's quest for a general who could command the Army of the Potomac with something comparable to the success being achieved by Grant in the West. The second was written to General George G. Meade who had in turn replaced Hooker. The envelope containing it bears Lincoln's endorsement "To Gen. Meade, never sent, or signed."

Executive Mansion,
Washington, January 26, 1863

Major General Hooker:
General.

I have placed you at the head of the Army of the

George G. Meade.

Potomac. Of course I have done this upon what
appear to me to be sufficient reasons. And yet I think
it best for you to know that there are some things in
regard to which, I am not quite satisfied with you.
I believe you to be a brave and skilful soldier, which,
of course, I like. I also believe you do not mix politics
with your profession, in which you are right. You
have confidence in yourself, which is a valuable, if
not an indispensable quality. You are ambitious
which, within reasonable bounds, does good rather
than harm. But I think that during General Burnside's
command of the Army, you have taken counsel of
your ambition, and thwarted him as much as you
could, in which you did a great wrong to the country,
and to a most meritorious and honorable brother
officer. I have heard, in such way as to believe it, of
your recently saying that both the Army and the

Government needed a Dictator. Of course it was not *for* this, but in spite of it, that I have given you the command. Only those generals who gain successes, can set up dictators. What I now ask of you is military success, and I will risk the dictatorship. The government will support you to the utmost of its ability, which is neither more nor less than it has done and will do for all commanders. I much fear that the spirit which you have aided to infuse into the Army, of criticising their Commander, and withholding confidence from him, will now turn upon you. I shall assist you as far as I can, to put it down. Neither you, nor Napoleon, if he were alive again, could get any good out of an army, while such a spirit prevails in it.

And now, beware of rashness. Beware of rashness, but with energy, and sleepless vigilance, go forward, and give us victories.

Yours very truly   A. Lincoln

Executive Mansion,
Washington, July 14, 1863.

Major General Meade

    I have just seen your despatch to General Halleck, asking to be relieved of your command, because of a supposed censure of mine. I am very – *very* – grateful to you for the magnificient success you gave the cause of the country at Gettysburg; and I am sorry now to be the author of the slightest pain to you. But I was in such deep distress myself that I could not restrain some expression of it. I had been oppressed nearly ever since the battles at Gettysburg, by what appeared to be evidences that yourself, and General Couch, and General Smith, were not seeking a collision with the enemy, but were trying to get him across the river without another battle. What these evidences were, if you please, I hope to tell you at some time, when we shall both feel better. The case, summarily stated, is this. You fought and beat the enemy at Gettysburg;

Scene of the Gettysburg Address.

and, of course, to say the least, his loss was as great as yours. He retreated; and you did not, as it seemed to me, pressingly pursue him; but a flood in the river detained him, till, by slow degrees, you were again upon him. You had at least twenty thousand veteran troops directly with you, and as many more raw ones within supporting distance, all in addition to those who fought with you at Gettysburg; while it was not possible that he had received a single recruit; and yet you stood and let the flood run down, bridges be built, and the enemy move away at his leisure, without attacking him. And Couch and Smith! The latter left Carlisle in time, upon all ordinary calculation, to have aided you in the last battle at Gettysburg; but he did not arrive. At the end of more than ten days, I believe twelve, under constant urging, he reached Hagerstown from Carlisle, which is not an inch over fiftyfive miles, if so much. And Couch's movement was very little different.

Again, my dear general, I do not believe you appreciate the magnitude of the misfortune involved in Lee's escape. He was within your easy grasp, and to have

156

closed upon him would, in connection with our other late successes, have ended the war. As it is, the war will be prolonged indefinitely. If you could not safely attack Lee last Monday, how can you possibly do so South of the river, when you can take with you very few more than two thirds of the force you then had in hand? It would be unreasonable to expect, and I do not expect you can now effect much. Your golden opportunity is gone, and I am distressed immeasurably because of it.

I beg you will not consider this a prosecution, or persecution of yourself. As you had learned that I was dissatisfied, I have thought it best to kindly tell you why.

But if such as these are the original gold nuggets of history, two of Lincoln's addresses remain the struck medallions, upon the matrices of which he spent all the art he knew how to bring to the engraving of an enduring work of art. The first would memorialize the Battle of Gettysburg as the agonizing rebirth of the nation, and the second would memorialize, also with backward glance and forward look, the end of a struggle and a career, which Lincoln's foreboding told him would cease almost together.

Address Delivered at the Dedication of
the Cemetery at Gettysburg
November 19, 1863

Four score and seven years ago our fathers brought forth on this continent, a new nation, conceived in Liberty, and dedicated to the proposition that all men are created equal.

Now we are engaged in a great civil war, testing whether that nation, or any nation so conceived and so dedicated, can long endure. We are met on a great battle-field of that war. We have come to dedicate a portion of that field, as a final resting place for those who here gave their lives that that nation might live. It is altogether fitting and proper that we should do this.

But, in a larger sense, we can not dedicate – we can not consecrate – we can not hallow – this ground. The brave men, living and dead, who struggled here, have consecrated it, far above our poor power to add or detract. The world will little note, nor long remember what we say here, but it can never forget what they did here. It is for us the living, rather to be dedicated here to the unfinished work which they who fought here have thus far so nobly advanced. It is rather for us to be here dedicated to the great task remaining before us – that from these honored dead we take increased devotion to that cause for which they gave the last full measure of devotion – that we here highly resolve that these dead shall not have died in vain – that this nation, under God, shall have a new birth of freedom – and that government of the people, by the people, for the people, shall not perish from the earth.

Second inaugural ceremony, March 4, 1865.

Second Inaugural Address

At this second appearing to take the oath of the presidential office, there is less occasion for an extended address than there was at the first. Then a statement, somewhat in detail, of a course to be pursued, seemed fitting and proper. Now, at the expiration of four years, during which public declarations have been constantly called forth on every point and phase of the great contest which still absorbs the attention, and engrosses the energies of the nation, little that is new could be presented. The progress of our arms, upon which all else chiefly depends, is as well known to the public as to myself; and it is, I trust, reasonably satisfactory and encouraging to all. With high hope for the future, no prediction in regard to it is ventured.

On the occasion corresponding to this four years ago, all thoughts were anxiously directed to an impending civil-war. All dreaded it – all sought to avert it. While the inaugural address was being delivered from this place, devoted altogether to *saving* the Union without war, insurgent agents were in the city seeking to *destroy* it without war – seeking to dissolve the Union, and divide effects, by negotiation. Both parties deprecated war; but one of them would *make* war rather than let the nation survive; and the other would *accept* war rather than let it perish. And the war came.

One eighth of the whole population were colored slaves, not distributed generally over the Union, but localized in the Southern part of it. These slaves constituted a peculiar and powerful interest. All knew that this interest was, somehow, the cause of the war. To strengthen, perpetuate, and extend this interest was

159

Second draft of the Gettysburg Address, from which Lincoln probably read at Gettysburg. →

the object for which the insurgents would rend the Union, even by war; while the government claimed no right to do more than to restrict the territorial enlargement of it. Neither party expected for the war, the magnitude, or the duration, which it has already attained. Neither anticipated that the *cause* of the conflict might cease with, or even before the conflict itself should cease. Each looked for an easier triumph, and a result less fundamental and astounding. Both read the same Bible, and pray to the same God; and each invokes His aid against the other. It may seem strange that any men should dare to ask a just God's assistance in wringing their bread from the sweat of other men's faces; but let us judge not that we be not judged. The prayers of both could not be answered; that of neither has been answered fully. The Almighty has His own purpose. "Woe unto the world because of offences! for it must needs be that offences come; but woe to that man by whom the offence cometh!" If we shall suppose that American Slavery is one of those offences which, in the providence of God, must needs come, but which, having continued through His appointed time, He now wills to remove, and that He gives to both North and South, this terrible war, as

ysburg Address

long remember, what we say here, but
never forget what they did here. It is
us, the living, rather to be dedicated
ew to the unfinished work, which they have,
us far, so nobly carried on. It is rather
us to be here dedicated to the great
task remaining before us— that from these
honored dead we take increased devotion
that
the cause for which they here gave
last full measure of devotion— that
here highly resolve that these dead
have not here died in vain; that the,
tion shall have a new birth of freedom,
nor that this government of the people, by
people, for the people, shall not perish
on this earth.

Lincoln and General Joseph Hooker reviewing the Army of the Potomac in April, 1863. Sketch by Edwin Forbes.

the woe due to those by whom the offence came, shall we discern therein any departure from those divine attributes which the believers in a Living God always ascribe to Him? Fondly do we hope – fervently do we pray – that this mighty scourge of war may speedily pass away. Yet, if God wills that it continue, until all the wealth piled by the bond-man's two hundred and fifty years of unrequited toil shall be sunk, and until every drop of blood drawn with the lash, shall be paid by another drawn with the sword, as was said three thousand years ago, so still it must be said "the judgments of the Lord, are true and righteous altogether."

With malice toward none; with charity for all; with firmness in the right, as God gives us to see the right, let us strive on to finsh the work we are in; to bind up the nation's wounds; to care for him who shall have borne the battle, and for his widow, and his orphan – to do all which may achieve and cherish a just, and a lasting peace, among ourselves, and with all nations.

162

9

The tone of Lincoln's Second Inaugural Address was in some measure a reflection of the President's physical condition, as well as his mental and emotional resignation to ultimate destiny. Horace Greeley described how Lincoln appeared at the time of an interview a few days later: "... his face was haggard with care and seamed with thought and trouble. It looked care-ploughed, tempest-tossed, and weatherbeaten." On March 14, Lincoln was so exhausted that he held his Cabinet meeting in his bedroom, but on March 20, when General Grant, anticipating that at long last the end was in sight, invited the President and Mrs. Lincoln to visit his headquarters, Lincoln accepted, traveling on the *River Queen* down the Potomac River and Chesapeake Bay and up the James River, to City Point, Virginia.

On March 28, Grant and Sherman, who had been summoned up from North Carolina, joined Lincoln in a final council of war held in the cabin of the *River Queen.*

Lincoln walks into Richmond.

Though the end was nearing, both generals agreed that probably one more bloody battle would have to be fought. Lincoln hoped it could be avoided. They discussed what to do with the Confederate armies and political leaders after surrender. Lincoln indicated his wish that the soldiers should be allowed to go home and get back to their peaceful occupations as soon as possible. As for the politicans, he was reminded of the old drunkard who had taken the pledge but hoped someone would "spike" his lemonade "unbeknownst." So he hoped Jefferson Davis would escape "unbeknownst to me."

On April 1 and 2, news came of the fall of Petersburg and the evacuation of Richmond. On April 4, the *River Queen* went up the James River, and Lincoln, accompanied by Admiral David D. Porter and a small guard of seamen, walked the two miles into the city, left shattered and burning by the retreating Confederates. As the word spread, both whites and Negroes lined the streets – whites in stunned but curious silence, Negroes jubilant. In the headquarters set up in President Jefferson Davis' house, Lincoln discussed with General Godfrey Weitzel the handling of the conquered people. Lincoln said, "I'd let 'em up easy, let 'em up easy."

Lincoln's return to Washington on the *River Queen* provided rest and relaxation. He read Shakespeare to pass the time, and at one point in *Macbeth* read aloud to the company:

> Duncan is in his grave;
> After life's fitful fever he sleeps well;
> Treason has done his worst: nor steel, nor poison,
> Malice domestic, foreign levy, nothing,
> Can touch him further!

In his own family and among those friends closest

165

"The Peace Makers," painting by George P. Healy, showing Lincoln with Generals Sherman and Grant and Admiral Porter in the cabin of the *"River Queen."*

Lincoln visits the late residence of Jefferson Davis (Frank Leslie's Illustrated Newspaper, *vol. 20*, p. *84, 1865).

to him, the President's forebodings of assassination had been common knowledge for four years, but in recent weeks had been of increasing intensity. A few days later, he recounted to a small group, including Mrs. Lincoln and his old friend and law partner Ward Hill Lamon, whom he had appointed Marshall of the District of Columbia, a strange dream which was, he said, "like Banquo's ghost, it will not down."

"About ten days ago," said he, "I retired very late. I had been up waiting for important dispatches from the front. I could not have been long in bed when I fell into a slumber, for I was weary. I soon began to dream. There seemed to be a deathlike stillness about me. Then I heard subdued sobs, as if a number of people were weeping. I thought I left my bed and wandered downstairs. There the silence was broken by the same pitiful sobbing, but the mourners were invisible. I went from room to room; no living person was in sight, but the same mournful sounds of distress met me as I passed along. It was light in all the rooms; every object was familiar to me; but where were all the people who were grieving as if their hearts would break? I was puzzled and alarmed. What could be the meaning of all this? Determined to find the cause of a state of things so mysterious and so shocking, I kept on until I arrived at the East Room, which I entered. There I met with a sickening surprise. Before me was a catafalque, on which rested a corpse wrapped in funeral vestments. Around it were stationed soldiers who were acting as guards; and there was a throng of people, some gazing mournfully upon the corpse, whose face was covered, others weeping pitifully. 'Who is dead in the White House?' I demanded of one of the soldiers. 'The President,' was his answer; 'he was killed by an assassin!' Then came a loud burst of grief from the crowd which awoke me from my dream. I slept no more that night; and although it was only a dream, I have been strangely annoyed by it ever since."

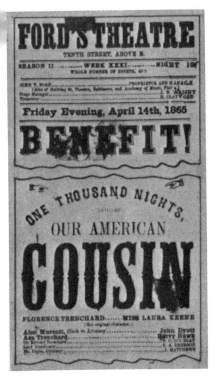

On Good Friday, April 14, Lincoln called a Cabinet meeting and invited General Grant to attend.

Bloodstained playbill picked up from the floor of Lincoln's box by William Hinkley Taylor.

Following Lee's surrender at Appomattox on April 9, he had daily hoped for news from General Sherman of the final capitulation in North Carolina of the last Confederate army in the field, and today felt certain that it would come. His reason for certainty was recorded by Secretary Welles in his diary.

The President remarked it would, no doubt, come soon, and come favorable, for he had last night the usual dream which he had preceding nearly every great and important event of the War. Generally the news had been favorable which succeeded this dream, and the dream itself was always the same. I inquired what this remarkable dream could be. He said it related to your (my) element, the water; that he seemed to be in some singular, indescribable vessel, and that he was moving with great rapidity toward an indef-

168

John Wilkes Booth.

inite shore; that he had this dream preceding Sumter, Bull Run, Antietam, Gettysburg, Stone River, Vicksburg, Wilmington, etc. General Grant said Stone River was certainly no victory, and he knew of no great results which followed from it. The President said however that might be, his dream preceded that fight.

"I had," the President remarked, "this strange dream again last night, and we shall, judging from the past, have great news very soon. I think it must be from Sherman. My thoughts are in that direction, as are most of yours."

"Every great and important event of the War" – but this time Lincoln would never know how clearly right though clearly wrong his foreboding would prove to be. Following the Cabinet meeting, he returned to his office to attend to routine business – signing papers and pardons, seeing callers, and whatever was to be done – and late in the afternoon went for a drive with Mary. He

The assassination (Currier & Ives).

169

Sketch made on the morning after Lincoln's death, by Hermann Faber, hospital steward.

had been much worried for her of late, as she was for him. Even the trip on the *River Queen* and visit at Grant's headquarters had produced an unpleasant incident, when Mary created a scene, accusing Mrs. Grant of scheming to succeed her in the White House. Although Grant had given politely acceptable reasons for his and Mrs. Grant's refusal of the President's invitation to accompany them to the theater that evening, there could be little doubt that there were other "difficulties" not mentioned between the two men.

John Wilkes Booth, an actor in quest of a degree of fame he could never achieve on any other stage, had also been busy that day, as for weeks before. All details of the plot had been carefully worked out with his fellow secessionist conspirators, and the time set. In the third act of the British farce *Our American Cousin*, Booth made his way through the familiar Ford's Theater to the President's box, handed a note to the President's coachman sitting near the door, entered quietly. Lincoln sat close to his wife, beside them their guests, Major Henry R. Rathbone and Miss Clara Harris, daughter of Senator Ira Harris of New York. Mary Lincoln affectionately held her husband's arm, whispering, "What will Miss Harris think of my hanging on to you so?" He replied, "She won't think anything about it." Booth stepped forward and placed a derringer behind the President's ear. The explosion was scarcely noticed by the audience, but Major Rathbone grappled with Booth and received a serious knife wound. Booth leaped from the box onto the stage, shouting "Sic Semper Tyrannis," the motto of the State of Virginia, limped off stage, out into the alley where he had tethered his horse, and escaped into the night.

Early the next morning Lincoln died in the house of William Peterson, a tailor who lived across the street from the theater. Secretary of War Stanton, who had once called Lincoln "the Illinois Ape," memorialized him in the moment after death with the utterance, "Now he belongs to the ages."

Ford's Theater draped in mourning.

Epilogue

What kind of man was Abraham Lincoln? Perhaps there can be no wholly satisfactory answer. Not only did he seem to be a different personality to people who knew him at different times and under differing circumstances, and who assessed him through their own ideas, emotions, and commitments, but also he became, and is perhaps still becoming, something different from the man even his most objectively perceptive contemporaries knew and judged. Like a character in one of his favorite Shakespearean plays, he was elected by a destiny within himself to do the things he wanted and deserved to do, knowing in part where they led, and at times foreboding even what he did not know. This may seem in the twentieth century merely the psychology of biography; what it may seem to the "science" of the future remains to be seen. But few men have either lived or written a story of imagination and achievement equal to the one Lincoln both lived and wrote. He sought through art to transcend life and succeeded through life in transcending art.

It is this reality of creative imagination which has made Lincoln the symbolic American hero of so many American poets from Whitman to Sandburg in our own day, and which Whitman expressed by saying, "What Shakespeare did in poetic expression, Abraham Lincoln essentially did in his personal and official life." Edwin Arlington Robinson apostrophized this quality of real imagination:

173

Lincoln as conceived by **Le Grelot**.

For we were not as other men:
'Twas ours to soar and his to see.
But we are coming down again,
And we shall come down pleasantly;
Nor shall we longer disagree
On what it is to be sublime
But flourish in our perigee
And have one Titan at a time.

So great had Lincoln's world stature become in death that by the tenth anniversary of his Gettysburg Address – perhaps with implications for the French Republic reborn following the Franco-Prussian War – the cartoonist in the Paris *Le Grelot*, November 23, 1873, depicted Lincoln as a giant dwarfing the Tom Thumb figure of Uncle Sam as a symbol of the nation that gave him birth. The role which Lincoln had sought to play, in a large measure created for himself as circumstance and opportunity arose, was thus rounded in his symbolic identity as a folk hero, in lands and among peoples who knew the United States chiefly, perhaps in some areas solely, as the Land of Lincoln, the man who had abolished slavery and saved his country.

Perhaps Lincoln's most appealing quality to men everywhere is the mystical certainty, the almost superstitious sureness with which he lived and acted in the midst of an overwhelming uncertainty that forced his candid recognition. "I claim not to have controlled events," he wrote to a newspaper editor on April 4, 1864, "but confess plainly that events have controlled me." And yet it is difficult to read his story without becoming, with him, convinced that within the framework of a free society and government "of the people, by the people, for the people," the individual makes his own destiny. "I am a living witness," he told a group of soldiers on August 22,

1864, "that any one of your children may look to come here as my father's child has." He believed what he said. This was why the principle of freedom *and* equality, though ambiguous, was what he called, quoting Scripture, "the apple of gold" in the "picture of silver."

Lincoln tomb, Springfield, Illinois.

Chronology

This brief chronology is based upon one prepared by Harry E. Pratt and published by the Illinois State Historical Library, Springfield, 1953. The monumental *Lincoln Day by Day* (3 vols., Washington, 1960-61), edited by Earl Schenk Miers, *et al*, for the Lincoln Sesquicentennial Commission, is available ($6.50) from the Superintendent of Documents, U. S. Government Printing Office, Washington 25, D. C.

1809

Feb. 12. "I was born Feb. 12, 1809, in Hardin County, Kentucky." The cabin on Nolin River was three miles south of present-day Hodgenville (now in LaRue County).

1811

Spring. Thomas Lincoln moves his family to a better farm of 230 acres on Knob Creek, ten miles north and six miles east of Hodgenville.

1815

Autumn. Before leaving Kentucky Abraham and his sister were sent for short periods to A.B.C. schools.

1816

Autumn. From the Knob Creek farm Thomas Lincoln removed to what is now Spencer County, Indiana, Abraham then being in his eighth year.

1817

Feb. Abraham took an early start as a hunter. A flock of wild turkeys approached the new log cabin, and Abraham shot through a crack, and killed one of them.

1818

Oct. 5. Abraham's mother, Nancy Hanks Lincoln, dies of "milk sickness."

1819

Dec. 2. Abraham's father, Thomas Lincoln, and Mrs. Sarah Bush Johnston are married in Elizabethtown, Kentucky.

1826

March. Spencer County. Abraham writes "1826" on a page of his "Book of Examples in Arithmetic."

1828

Jan. 20. Sarah Lincoln Grigsby, sister of Abraham, dies in childbirth in her twenty-first year.

Autumn. Abraham makes his first trip upon a flatboat to New Orleans.

1830

Mar. 1. Thomas Lincoln's family and the families of Mrs. Lincoln's two sons-in-law, a party of thirteen persons, start for Illinois. Abraham drives one of the ox-wagons.

Mar. 15. The Lincoln party arrives at Decatur, Illinois, and Abraham's father establishes a new home eight miles southwest of town on the Sangamon River.

1831

March. Lincoln helps build a flatboat at Sangamon Town, seven miles northwest of Springfield.

Apr.-July. Lincoln pilots the flatboat with produce of Denton Offutt to New Orleans and returns to New Salem, eighteen miles northwest of Springfield.

Aug. 1. Lincoln casts his first vote and gains a reputation as a storyteller; and a month later becomes a store clerk.

1832

Mar. 9. Lincoln announces his candidacy for the legislature.

Apr. 7. Lincoln is elected a captain in the 31st Regiment Illinois Militia.

Apr. 21. Lincoln is elected captain of a volunteer company enlisted for thirty days to drive Black Hawk and his band west of the Mississippi River.

May 27. Lincoln is mustered out and re-enlists as a private in Captain Elijah Iles' company for twenty days.

June 16. Lincoln re-enlists for thirty days in Captain Jacob M. Early's Independent Spy Corps.

July 10. Lincoln writes the mustering out roll for Captain Early. It is certified by Lieutenant Robert Anderson, who commanded at Fort Sumter in 1861.

Aug. 6. Lincoln is defeated for the legislature in today's election, the "only time I have been beaten by the people." He runs eighth in a field of thirteen candidates.

1833

Jan. 15. William F. Berry and Lincoln purchase the New Salem store formerly owned by Reuben Radford, but they go "deeper and deeper in debt. . . . The store winked out."

May 7. Lincoln is appointed postmaster of New Salem by President Jackson. He serves until the post office is moved to Petersburg on May 30, 1836.

1834

Jan. 6. Lincoln's first survey, as a deputy surveyor of Sangamon

County, is of 800 acres for Reason Shipley. He continues his surveying until the end of 1836.

Aug. 4. Lincoln is elected one of four Sangamon County members of the lower house of the Illinois General Assembly. He is re-elected for the next three terms.

Sept. 30. Lincoln makes his first town survey, New Boston on the Mississippi. In 1836 he surveys Petersburg, Huron, Albany and Bath.

1835

Aug. 25. Lincoln's legendary sweetheart, Ann Rutledge, dies at the farm home seven miles northwest of New Salem.

1837

Jan.-Feb. Lincoln and the other members of the "Long Nine" from Sangamon County cast their votes for the internal improvements bill, and Lincoln's skill gets the state capital moved from Vandalia to Springfield.

Mar. 3. Lincoln and Dan Stone enter their protest in the *House Journal* against the anti-Abolitionist resolutions adopted on January 20. Their real difference from the House view was moral – the injustice of slavery.

Apr. 15. Lincoln, admitted to the bar March 1, moves to Springfield, rooms with Joshua F. Speed, and becomes the law partner of John T. Stuart in the firm of Stuart & Lincoln.

1838

Dec. 3. Lincoln is beaten for speaker of the House at the opening of the Eleventh General Assembly. He is again beaten in the Twelfth (1840). He serves as Whig floor leader.

1839

June 24. Lincoln begins a year's service as a member of the Board of Trustees of the town of Springfield.

Sept. 23. Lincoln begins practice on the newly organized Eighth Judicial Circuit. He continues to attend these courts until his nomination for the presidency.

Oct. 8. Lincoln is chosen one of the presidential electors by the Whig convention. He is likewise honored in 1844, 1852, and 1856.

1841

Jan. 1. Lincoln calls this "the fatal 1st. of Jan'y. 1841," when an emotional crisis upsets his relations with Mary Todd, and causes him acute mental anguish.

Apr. 14. The partnership of Stuart & Lincoln is dissolved and Lincoln becomes the junior partner of Stephen T. Logan.

Aug.-Sept. Lincoln visits three weeks with his intimate friend Joshua Speed, at his country home, Farmington, near Louisville, Kentucky.

1842

Sept. 22. Lincoln's proposed duel with James Shields is averted when, without Shields' knowledge, his friends withdraw his note to Lincoln and read Lincoln's apology

Nov. 4. Lincoln and Mary Todd are married in the evening at the home of her brother-in-law, Ninian W. Edwards, by the Rev. Charles Dresser, minister of the Episcopal Church.

Aug. 1. Robert Todd Lincoln, first child of the Lincolns, is born at the Globe Tavern, where they are then residing.

1844

May 2. The Lincolns move from a cottage on South Fourth Street into the house at Eighth and Jackson streets, their home until they go to the White House.

Oct. 30. Lincoln speaks at Rockport, Indiana, near his boyhood home, at the close of his campaign tour of southern Illiniois, Kentucky and Indiana, for Henry Clay.

Dec. 9. William H. Herndon is admitted to the bar. The firm of Lincoln & Herndon is organized soon afterward.

1846

Mar. 10. Edward Baker Lincoln, second child of the Lincolns, is born and named for Edward Dickinson Baker, a friend and political associate.

Aug. 3. Lincoln is the only Whig among seven congressmen in Illinois elected today. His majority of 1,511 votes over the Rev. Peter Cartwright is unprecedented.

1847

Oct. 25. The Lincolns and their two boys start for Washington by way of Mary Todd Lincoln's girldhood home, Lexington, Kentucky.

Dec. 6. Lincoln takes his seat in the Thirtieth Congress, the only Congress of which he was a member.

Dec. 22. Lincoln presents a series of resolutions requesting President Polk to inform the House whether the "spot" where American blood was first shed in the Mexican War was not within territory claimed by Mexico.

1848

June 7-9. Lincoln attends his first national Whig convention, at Philadelphia, and is pleased with the nomination of General Zachary Taylor for President.

Sept. 12-22. Lincoln concludes a summer of campaign labor in and around Washington with a ten-day speaking tour in New England.

1849

Mar. 10. Lincoln applies for a patent on "a new and improved manner of combining adjustable buoyant chambers with steam boats or other vessels." The patent is granted on May 22.

June 21. Lincoln fails to get the appointment as commissioner of the General Land Office, for which he has made a special trip to Washington.

Aug. 21. Lincoln declines appointment as secretary of Oregon Territory.

Sept. 27. Lincoln declines appointment as governor of Oregon Territory.

1850

Feb. 1. Edward Baker Lincoln dies after being "sick fifty-two days."

Dec. 21. William Wallace Lincoln, third son of the Lincolns, is born.

1851

Jan. 17. Lincoln's father, Thomas, born in Virginia in 1778, dies in Coles County, Illinois.

1852

July 6. Lincoln delivers a eulogy on Henry Clay, his "beau ideal" of a statesman.

Aug. 14. Lincoln opens his speaking campaign for Winfield Scott for President with an attack upon Stephen A. Douglas' speech at Richmond, Virginia.

183

1853

Apr. 4. Thomas (Tad) Lincoln, fourth son of the Lincolns, is born.

1854

May 30. The Kansas-Nebraska Act is passed. Lincoln wrote in 1859: "From 1849 to 1854, both inclusive, practiced law more assiduously than ever before. . . . I was losing interest in politics, when the repeal of the Missouri Compromise aroused me again."

Oct. 16. Lincoln delivers at Peoria one of his first great speeches – on "the repeal of the Missouri Compromise, and the propriety of its restoration."

Nov. 7. Lincoln is elected to the Illinois legislature. He declines the office on November 27 in order to become a candidate for the U. S. Senate.

1855

Feb. 8. Lincoln fails of election to the U. S. Senate. To forestall election by the General Assembly of Joel A. Matteson he throws his votes to Lyman Trumbull to elect him on the tenth ballot.

1856

May 29. Lincoln delivers his famous "Lost Speech" at the organization of the Republican Party at Bloomington, Illinois. A presidential elector for the fourth time, he "made over fifty speeches" during the campaign.

June 19. Lincoln receives 110 votes on the first ballot for Vice-President at the first Republican National Convention in Philadelphia.

Aug. 27. Lincoln makes his only speech in Michigan, for Frémont, to a crowd of 10,000 at Kalamazoo.

Dec. 1. Lincoln presides over the Sangamon County Circuit Court in the absence of Judge David Davis. In later years he presides in at least four other counties.

1857

June 26. Lincoln delivers in Springfield his first major speech against the Dred Scott decision. He maintains that it was "erroneous," and urges that it not be accepted as a precedent.

Aug. 12. Lincoln receives his largest legal fee, $5,000, for winning Illinois Central Railroad *v.* County of McLean.

1858

June 16. "Abraham Lincoln is the first and only choice of the Republicans of Illinois for the United States Senate." Lincoln accepts the nomination and delivers the famous "House Divided" speech in the Hall of the House of Representatives of the state-house (present Sangamon County Courthouse).

Aug. 21-Oct. 15. The Lincoln-Douglas debates are held at Ottawa, Freeport, Jonesboro, Charleston, Galesburg, Quincy, and Alton.

Nov. 2. Lincoln gets a majority of the votes, but the gerrymandered legislative districts give Douglas his re-election to the U. S. Senate. Lincoln writes to a disheartened friend: "Quit that. You will soon feel better. Another 'blow-up' is coming; and we shall have fun again."

1859

Feb. 11. Lincoln delivers his lecture on the subject of "Discoveries and Inventions," in Jacksonville.

Sept. 16-17. Lincoln speaks twice in Columbus, Ohio, and in Dayton, Hamilton and Cincinnati.

Sept. 30. Lincoln addresses the Wisconsin State Fair at Milwaukee. He makes a political speech there in the evening, and in Beloit and Janesville the day following.

D.c. 1-3. Lincoln speaks in Kansas, at Elwood, Troy, Doniphan, Atchison and Leavenworth a few days before the territorial election.

1860

Feb. 27. Lincoln delivers his famous Cooper Union Address in New York City, which is printed in full by the New York *Tribune.*

185

Feb. 28. Lincoln begins a two-week speaking tour of New England. Included in the eleven speeches is one at Exeter, New Hampshire, where Robert Lincoln is attending Phillips Exeter Academy.

May 9-10. Lincoln attends the State Republican Convention at Decatur. The convention instructs the Illinois delegation for Lincoln the "Rail Splitter" for President.

May 18. Lincoln is nominated for President of the United States on the third ballot at the Republican National Convention in Chicago. Hannibal Hamlin of Maine is nominated for Vice-President.

Nov. 6. Lincoln is the first Republican to be elected President of the United States, defeating Douglas (Northern Democrat), John C. Breckinridge (Southern Democrat), and John Bell (Constitutional Unionist).

Dec. 20. South Carolina is the first Southern state to secede, and meets with five others (Texas not represented) on February 4, 1861, at Montgomery, Alabama, to form the Confederates States of America, with Jefferson Davis as president and Alexander H. Stephens as vice-president.

1861

Jan. 31. Lincoln goes to Coles County to visit his aged stepmother.

Feb. 11. Lincoln delivers his "Farewell Address" to the people of Springfield at the Great Western Railroad station.

Feb. 23. Lincoln arrives secretly in Washington after a twelve-day trip and many public appearances and speeches.

Mar. 4. Lincoln is inaugurated the Sixteenth President of the United States.

Apr. 12-14. Fort Sumter is attacked, and after thirty-four hours of bombardment, surrenders to the Confederate forces and is evacuated.

Apr. 15. Lincoln convenes an extra session of Congress to meet on July 4, and calls for 75,000 volunteers. Thereupon four border states secede.

Apr. 19, 27. Lincoln proclaims blockade of the Confederate states from Virginia to Texas.

May 3. The President's proclamation calls for 500,000 volunteers,

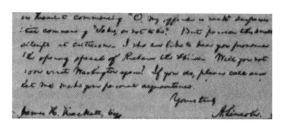

to which 700,680 respond. He also increases the regular Army and the Navy.

June 3. Stephen A. Douglas dies in Chicago at the age of forty-eight. His stirring address in Springfield, April 25, had united Illinois and encouraged thousands to enter the Union Army.

July 2. Lincoln suspends the writ of habeas corpus from Philadelphia to New York. On May 10 he had done this for portion of the Florida coast.

July 21. The President, Congress, and the North are shocked by the defeat of General Irvin McDowell's army at Bull Run.

July 22. Congress votes $500,000,000 to support the war, and gives Lincoln war powers.

July 27. Lincoln brings General George B. McClellan to Washington to command all the forces there and the Army of the Potomac.

Sept. 11. Lincoln revokes Frémont emancipation proclamation, thus bringing a storm of abuse from the antislavery faction.

Nov. 1. General Winfield Scott's resignation is accepted and McClellan is made commander-in-chief.

Nov. 8. Mason and Slidell, Confederate commissioners to Great Britain and France, are seized on the British steamer *Trent.*

Dec. 10. Congress resolves on the appointment of a joint committee to inquire into the conduct of the war.

Dec. 28. Mason and Slidell are surrendered to the British authorities by the government.

1862

Jan. 13. Lincoln sends Simon Cameron as minister to Russia, and replaces him with Edwin M. Stanton as Secretary of War.

Feb. 6, 16. Fort Henry on the Tennessee River and Fort Donelson on the Cumberland are taken by forces under General Grant, the first important victories of Northern armies.

Feb. 20. William Wallace Lincoln, eleven-year-old son of the President, dies. His death and the illness of his younger brother, Tad, prostrate Mrs. Lincoln.

Mar. 8-9. The Confederate ironclad *Merrimac* destroys the Northern ships in Hampton Roads, but Union ironclad *Monitor* forces it to retire.

Apr. 2. McClellan arrives at Fortress Monroe to begin a four-month campaign on the Virginia Peninsula.

Apr. 6-7. The Confederate attack at Pittsburg Landing or Shiloh, Tennessee, is repulsed with serious losses by both armies.

Apr. 25. New Orleans is captured by a Northern naval expedition under Admiral David G. Farragut.

May 15. Lincoln approves the act establishing the Department of Agriculture.

May 20. Lincoln signs the Homestead Law, which grants a quarter section of unoccupied land to homesteaders on payment of nominal fees after five years of actual residence.

June 20. Slavery is prohibited in the territories by act of Congress.

July 1. Lincoln approves the Union Pacific Railroad Company charter.

July 2. The Morrill Agricultural College Land Grant Act becomes a law. Battles of the Seven Days culminate in the retreat of the Army of the Potomac.

July 11. Lincoln appoints General Henry W. Halleck general-in-chief.

July 17. Congress authorizes a draft of state militia, and empowers the President to accept Negroes for military and naval service.

Aug. 30. Northern forces under General John Pope are defeated at Bull Run.

Sept. 2. Lincoln removes Pope and places McClellan in command of all troops around Washington.

Sept. 17. McClellan stops General Robert E. Lee's Northern invasion in the Battle of Antietam or Sharpsburg, Maryland.

Sept. 22. President Lincoln issues preliminary proclamation of emancipation of slaves of rebels, to take effect January 1, 1863.

188

Sept. 24. Lincoln suspends the writ of habeas corpus for all persons arrested by military authority.

Oct. 2. Lincoln visits the battlefield of Antietam.

Dec. 13. The Army of the Potomac under command of General Ambrose E. Burnside is defeated at Fredericksburg, Virginia.

Dec. 31. Lincoln reluctantly approves the bill admitting West Virginia to the Union.

1863

Jan. 1. Lincoln issues the Emancipation Proclamation whereby slaves in areas held by Confederates are declared free.

Feb. 25. Congress establishes a national currency; the National Bank Act is passed.

Mar. 3. Lincoln approves the first draft law in the nation's history.

May 2-4. The Army of the Potomac commanded by General Joseph Hooker is defeated at Chancellorsville, Virginia.

July 1-3. The Confederate invasion of Pennsylvania under Lee is defeated by General George G. Meade at Gettysburg.

July 4. The long siege of Vicksburg by Grant results in the surrender of the Confederates under General John C. Pemberton.

Sept. 20. The Northern defeat at Chickamauga is offset five days later by victory at Chattanooga.

Nov. 19. Lincoln delivers his dedicatory address at the Gettysburg Cemetery.

Nov. 26. First national observance of Thanksgiving is ordered by the President.

Dec. 8. Lincoln issues a proclamation of amnesty to Confederates who take the oath of allegiance.

1864

Mar. 12. The President appoints Ulysses S. Grant, who had become a lieutenant general on March 9, general-in-chief of the armies.

May 5-12. Grant and Lee are in constant battle in the Virginia Wilderness.

189

June 7. The National Union Convention at Baltimore renominates Lincoln for President; Andrew Johnson of Tenessee is nominated for Vice-President.

June 28. Congress repeals the Fugitive Slave Law.

July 4. Lincoln pocket vetoes the drastic congressional Reconstruction bill.

Sept. 2. General William T. Sherman takes Atlanta, a Northern victory which, with that of Farragut at Mobile Bay on August 5, insures Lincoln's re-election. Invasion of eastern Tennessee, long sought by Lincoln, becomes a reality with the occupation of Knoxville.

Nov. 8. Lincoln is re-elected President.

Nov. 21. Lincoln writes a letter of sympathy to Mrs. Lydia Bixby, who he was incorrectly informed had lost five sons in battle.

Dec. 10. Sherman's march "from Atlanta to the sea" concludes at Savannah, Georgia, which surrenders on December 21.

1865

Feb. 1. Lincoln approves the Thirteenth Amendment, abolishing slavery.

Feb. 3. Lincoln attends an unsuccessful peace conference at Hampton Roads, Virginia.

Mar. 3. The Freedmen's Bureau is established by Congress to care for the Negroes.

Mar. 4. Lincoln is re-inaugurated and delivers his Second Inaugural Address.

Mar. 5. The first Negro entertained at the White House is Frederick Douglass.

Mar. 22-Apr. 6. Lincoln visits Grant's army at City Point, Virginia.

Apr. 4-5. Lincoln goes to see the ruins of the evacuated city of Richmond.

Apr. 9. Lee surrenders to Grant at Appomattox Court House, Virginia.

Apr. 11. Lincoln delivers his last speech, from a window of the White House, in response to a serenade.

April. 14. Lincoln is shot at Ford's Theater by the actor John Wilkes Booth.

Apr. 15. Abraham Lincoln dies at 7:22 a.m. and the country goes into mourning.

Apr. 19. Funeral services for President Lincoln are held in the White House.

Apr. 21-May 3. The funeral train bears the remains of Lincoln on the journey to Springfield, Illinois.

A Bibliographical Note

From the excellent bibliographies given in each of the few works which are here suggested, the reader can learn about the thousands of books on Abraham Lincoln, and can allow his appetite and digestion to determine the extent of his feast. Among one volume, full-length biographies, incomparably the best is: Benjamin P. Thomas, *Abraham Lincoln, a Biography,* Alfred A. Knopf, New York, 1952. Of longer works, the following are recommended: Albert J. Beveridge, *Abraham Lincoln 1809-1858,* 2 vols. (also in 4 vols.), Houghton Mifflin, Boston and New York, 1928; William H. Herndon and Jesse W. Weik, *Herndon's Lincoln, the True Story of a Great Life,* 2 vols., Chicago, 1889 (later reprintings by various publishers); John G. Nicolay and John Hay, *Abraham Lincoln, a History,* 10 vols., The Century Co., New York, 1890; James G. Randall, *Lincoln the President: Springfield to Gettysburg* (2 vols.), *Midstream* (1 vol.), *Last Full Measure* (1 vol., completed by Richard N. Current), Dodd, Mead & Co., New York, 1945, 1952, 1955; Carl Sandburg, *Abraham Lincoln: The Prairie Years* (2 vols.), *The War Years* (4 vols.), Harcourt, Brace & Co., New York, 1926, 1939.

No biography, however, can do as much as Lincoln's own works to set forth the mind and heart of the man: *The Collected Works of Abraham Lincoln,* Roy P. Basler, Editor, Marion Dolores Pratt and Lloyd A. Dunlap, Assistant Editors, 8 vols. and Index, Rutgers University Press, New Brunswick, N. J., 1953, 1955. A one volume selection, edited by Roy P. Basler, with critical and

191

analytical notes and a Preface by Carl Sandburg, is *Abraham Lincoln: His Speeches and Writings,* World Publishing Co., Cleveland and New York, 1946. Also a good volume of selections excerpted from *The Collected Works* is Paul M. Angle and Earl Schenk Miers, *The Living Lincoln,* Rutgers University Press, New Brunswick, N. J., 1955.

The military aspect of Lincoln's presidency, to which so little space could be devoted in a profile treatment, is ably presented by Colin R. Ballard, *The Military Genius of Abraham Lincoln,* Oxford University Press, London, 1926 (first American edition, World Publishing Co., Cleveland and New York, 1952), and T. Harry Williams, *Lincoln and His Generals,* Alfred A. Knopf, New York, 1952.

Acknowledgments

Chapter I, "Lincoln Country," is an abridgment of the author's "The Pioneering Period," which appeared in *The Centennial Review of the Arts and Sciences,* Vol. II, No. 2, Spring, 1958.

Illustrations: Library of Congress: 7, 14-15, 17, 34, 38, 40-41, 43, 45, 60, 66, 76, 77, 78, 81, 82-83, 86-87, 88, 90, 92, 95, 96-97, 100, 101, 102-103, 106, 107, 108, 112-113, 116, 117, 118, 119, 120, 122, 123, 124-125, 127, 128, 131, 132, 133, 139, 142-143, 145, 147, 149, 151, 153, 154-155, 156, 158, 160-161, 162, 163, 166, 167, 168, 169, 170, 171, 174, 178, 179, 180, 182, 184, 185, 186, 187, 188, 189, front cover, inside covers. Illinois State Historical Library 20, 23, 46-47, 56-57, 65, 135, 172, 181, 183. U. S. Information Agency: 4, 10, 114, 176. National Park Service: 19. Chicago Historical Society: 27, 30-31. Smithsonian Institution: 49. University of Nebraska: 50. Lincoln Memorial University: 52. Langston Hughes and Milton Meltzer, *A Pictorial History of the American Negro* © 1956: 69. C. Frank Reavis: 72. Oliver R. Barrett: 85, 111, 140. National Archives: 129. National Gallery of Art: 164.